2nd edition

W0018774

openMind

Workbook

Ingrid Wisniewska

Concept development:
Mariela Gil Vierma

MACMILLAN

Level 1

Macmillan Education
4 Crinan Street
London N1 9XW
A division of Macmillan Publishers Limited

Companies and representatives throughout the world

ISBN 978-0-230-45769-0 with key
ISBN 978-0-230-45920-5 without key

Text, design and illustration © Macmillan Publishers Limited 2014
Written by Ingrid Wisniewska
Additional material by Angela Hewitt

This edition published 2014
First edition published 2010

All rights reserved; no part of this publication may be reproduced, stored in a retrieval system, transmitted in any form, or by any means, electronic, mechanical, photocopying, recording, or otherwise, without the prior written permission of the publishers.

Designed by emc design Ltd
Illustrated by Peter Cornwell pp35, 44, 49, 54; Sally Elford pp27, 29, 38, 46; Mo Choy Design Ltd. pp31, 40, 55; Paul Williams (Sylvie Poggio Artists) pp6, 11, 15, 19, 34, 43, 56, 59, 61, 67
Photographic research: Susannah Jayes
Cover concept: Tony Richardson
The author and publishers would like to thank the following for permission to reproduce their photographs:
Cover Images: Corbis/Ted Levine

The authors would like to thank the schools, teachers and students whose input has been invaluable in preparing this new edition. They would also like to thank the editorial and design teams at Macmillan for doing such a great job of organizing the material and bringing it to life.

The publishers would like to thank the following educators and institutions who reviewed materials and provided us with invaluable insight and feedback for the development of the Open Mind series:
Carolina Ezeta, Universidad Tecnológica de Querétaro; Karl Schmack, Centro Cultural Costarricense Norteamericano; Maria Elisabeth Schmid de Mattos, ICBEU -São José dos Campos; Martha Patricia Sánchez, Colegio Anahuac Revolución; Leigh Darlaine Langenegger, ICBEU -São José dos Campos; Ricardo Pizelli Goiatá, Curso Bridge over Cam; Franklin Téllez, Centro Cultural Nicaragüense Norteamericano; Jim Nixon, Colegio Cervantes Costa Rica; Rosario Mena, Instituto Cultural Dominico Americano; Leticia de la Peña, Colegio Lincoln; Héctor Sánchez, PROULEX; Eric Tejeda, PROULEX; Arturo Hernández, Instituto Tecnológico de Estudios Superiores de Monterrey, Campus Guadalajara; Grisel del Rosario, Instituto Cultural Dominico Americano; Maria do Socorro Guimarães, IBEU -Rio de Janeiro; Diego Medina, Universidad de Guadalajara, Licenciatura de Idiomas; Julio Prin, Centro Venezolano Americano; María Guadalupe Muñoz, Universidad de Guadalajara, Licenciatura de Idiomas; Lourdes Molleda, Tec Milenio; Frances Gritzewsky, Prepa Tec Eugenio Garza; Magneli Villanueva Morales, Universidad Regiomontana; Anderson Lopes Siqueira, ICBEU -São José dos Campos; Emilia Rubenova, Universidad Autónoma de Nuevo León; Lourdes Pérez Valdespino, Universidad Del Valle de México, María Eugenia Rodríguez, Centro Cultural Salvadoreño Americano; Márcia Soares Guimarães, Instituto Cultural Brasil Estados Unidos -Belo Horizonte; Leonor Rosales, Instituto Tecnológico de Estudios Superiores de Monterrey; Martha Larraga, Unitec Escobedo; Cândido Prado, CCBEU – Goiânia; Janet Keyser, Instituto Tecnológico de Estudios Superiores de Monterrey, Campus Cuidad de México; Julie Khatcherian, Manhattan Trade Language Company; Francisco Nieto, Universidad Metropolitana; Artemisa Sangermán, Instituto Tecnológico de Estudios Superiores de Monterrey, Campus Cuidad de México; Nico Wieserma, Instituto Tecnológico de Estudios Superiores de Monterrey, Campus Cuidad de México; Vagner Serafim, Centro Cultural Brasil Estados Unidos; Lourdes Baledón, Universidad Intercontinental; Clara Lucía López, Centro Colombo Americano Manizales; Gabriela Rodríguez, Colegio Oviedo Schontal; Waldo Andrade, CBI: Centro Butantã Idiomas – São Paulo; Anthony Shull, Instituto Tecnológico de Estudios Superiores de Monterrey, Campus Estado de México; Tamara Rojas, Escuela Benjamín Franklin; Martha Rosas, Universidad del Valle de México, Campus San Rafael; Fabiano Cella, Universidade de São Paulo, curso Poliglota; Sheila Moreno, Universidad del Valle de México, Campus Tlalpan; Patricia Venegas, Universidad del Valle de México, Campus Lomas Verdes; Luciana Guarnier, Seven Idiomas; Diana Jones, Angloamericano; Carlos Lizárraga, Angloamericano; Emma Domínguez, The Anglo; Luis Cabrera, Universidad Nacional Autónoma de México; Luciane Oliveira, New York School; Cristina Moya, Colegio Morelos; Elda Beraza, Colegio Montes de Oca, Cuernavaca; Elza Massae Sato, FMU, São Paulo; Lucía Canseco Campoy, Instituto Tecnológico de Estudios Superiores de Monterrey, Campus Hermosillo; Emma Luisa Domínguez Instituto Tecnológico de Estudios Superiores de Monterrey, Campus Obregón; Yolanda Domínguez del Instituto Tecnológico de Estudios Superiores de Monterrey, Campus Obregón; Maria Antonieta Gagliardi, Centro Británico - São Paulo; David Toledo, Universidad Autónoma de Baja California; Alicia Cabrero, Universidad Autónoma San Luis Potosí; Danielle Sales, Senac – Rio de Janeiro; Claudio Barros, Flex Idiomas; Rina de Góngora, del Instituto Guatemalteco Americano; Adriana Alcalá, Kate Cory-Wright, Chris Bauer; Moisés Ramírez; Universidad Chauhtémoc Centro de Lenguas y Lingüística Aplicada, Universidad Autonoma de Tamaulipas; Instituto Tecnológico Centro Americano; CELE Mascarones; Ministerio de Educación de El Salvador; Universidad Tecnológica de Nezahualcoyotl; Universidad del Tepeyac; Instituto Politécnico Nacional ESIME CELEX; Instituto Quebec; Colegio La Salle del Pedregal; Universidad Pedagógica Nacional; Universidad de la República Mexicana; Universidad Norteamericana; Fundación Empresarial para el Desarrollo Educativo; Operadora La Salle; Seven São Paulo; Universidad de Oriente; UNIVA; Centro de Capacitación Manuel Sandoval Vallarta; Universidad de El Salvador; Escuela de Jurisprudencia; Universidad de Valle de México, Campus Puebla; Alumni São Paulo; Dr Amany Shawkey, Mrs Heidi Omara, Mrs Hala Fouad (Egypt); Faisal Mreish (Lebanon); Mrs Magda Giomazi (Libya). Petra Florianová, Gymnázium, Praha 6, Arabská 14; Inés Frigerio, Universidad Nacional de Río Cuarto; Alison Greenwood, University of Bologna, Centro Linguistico di Ateneo; Roumyana Yaneva Ivanova, The American College of Sofia; Táña Jančaříková, SOŠ Drtinova Prague; Mari Carmen Lafuente, Escuela Oficial de Idiomas Hospitalet, Barcelona; Alice Lockyer, Pompeu Fabra University; Javier Roque Sandro Majul, Windmill School of English; Paul Neale, Susan Carol Owens and Beverley Anne Sharp, Cambridge Academy of English; Audrey Renton, Dubai Men's College, Higher Colleges of Technology, UAE; Martin Stanley, British Council, Bilbao; Luiza Wójtowicz-Waga, Warsaw Study Centre; Escuela Oficial de Idiomas de Getxo; Cámara de Comercio de Bilbao; Universidad Autónoma de Bellaterra; Escuela Oficial de Idiomas EOI de Barcelona; University of Barcelona; Escuela Oficial de Idiomas Sant Gervasi.

The authors and publishers would like to thank the following for permission to reproduce their photographs:
Alamy/Beyond Fotomedia GmbH p5(tr), David Burton p21(5), Nick Cleave Photography p10(A), BRUCE COLEMAN INC. p64(cr), Tony Cordoza p21(6), Cultura Creative (RF) p71(bcm), directphoto.bz p72, imagebroker pp14,21(3),74(tcmr), Evgeny Karandaev p47(4), Chris Kelly p47(3), MBI p24, PHOVOIR p42(cr), M.Sobreira p21(4), Hugh Threlfall p47(2), Wavebreak Media ltd p13, szefei wong p5(cml); **Apple Computers**/Courtesy Apple Computers p47(1); **BananaStock** p44(tmr); **Brand X** pp10(E),36(tr),47(5),52(8),69(1); **Comstock Images** pp44(tl),52(1,4,9); **Corbis**/Benelux p71(tr), Heide Benser p12, Bettmann p68, Erik Isakson/Blend Images p42(cm), Andersen Ross/Blend Images p26, Don Hammond/Design Pics p69(3), ©Emmanuel Dunand/epa p64(tl), David Spurdens/www.ExtremeSportsPhoto.com p18, Hulton-Deutsch Collection p64(cl), Ed Kashi p65(b), moodboard p69(2), Ocean p44(tr), Tim Pannell p4, Douglas Peebles p58, Studio Eye p60; **Getty Images** p52(7,10,13), Apelöga p8, Gonzalo Azumendi p33(4,5), John W Banagan p63, Paul Bernhardt p71(bcr), Michael Blann p21(7), Anders Blomqvist p71(tl), zhang bo p7, Greg Ceo p46(tr), Design Pics/Deddeda p67, Gordon Dixon p10(B), Emilio Ereza p21(1), French School p10(F), Don Fuchs p74(t), Fuse pp5(tcr),44(tml), Glow Cuisine p54(2), Rubberball/Mike Kemp p41, Paul Kennedy p29, Christian Kober p28, Rob Lawson p47(cl), Siegfried Layda p33(1), Ron Levine p16(tmr), Lonely Planet p33(3), Ghislain & Marie David de Lossy p71(bcl), Zoran Milich p10(C), Moment p46(tmr), Medioimages/Photodisc p9, John Lund/Marc Romanelli p23, Felix Sanchez p16(tr), Luca Trovato p54(1), Andrew Unangst p47(cr), Design Pics/Sean White p74(cr); **Macmillan Publishers Ltd**/Paul Bricknell p52(6), Rob Judges/Des Dubber p10(D), David Tolley/Dean Ryan p30, David Tolley p52(5); **Photoalto** p57; **Photodisc** p17, Photodisc/Getty Images p52(3); **Photoshot** p33(2), NHPA p65(tr); **Press Association**/Steve Parsons/PA Archive p64(bcl); **Rex Features**/Tom Dymond p64(bcr), ©Sony Pics/Everett p75(cr), Warner Br./Everett p73, ©Weinstein/Everett p75(tr), ITV p64(tr), Snap Stills p75(br); **Superstock**/Asia Images p42(cl); **Thinkstock**/Istockphoto pp21(2),32,36(C),47(cm), 50,52(11,12),p54(3,4), George Doyle/Stockbyte p52(2).

This material may contain links for third-party websites. We have no control over, and are not responsible for, the contents of such third-party websites. Please use care when accessing them.

Although we have tried to trace and contact copyright holders before publication, in some cases this has not been possible. If contacted we will be pleased to rectify any errors or omissions at the earliest opportunity.

Printed and bound in Thailand

2018 2017 2016 2015 2014
10 9 8 7 6 5 4 3 2 1

CONTENTS

UNIT 1 NICE TO MEET YOU!

1 READING: recognizing cognates

A Read the text. Circle the cognates.

My name is Pierre Boisseau. I speak French, English, and Spanish. I'm a student at Miami University, and I study computer science. I have a part-time job in a computer store. My interests are video games, music, and movies. I also love sports, especially soccer. My best friend is Victor Martinez. We are in the same class. Our teacher is Professor Wilson.

B Match the words from the text to the correct meaning.

1	French	a)	a sport
2	science	b)	a free-time activity
3	university	c)	a language
4	soccer	d)	an academic subject
5	video games	e)	a group of students
6	class	f)	a place of college study

C Write four more English words that are cognates in your language.

1 _____   3 _____

2 _____   4 _____

2 VOCABULARY: useful questions

A 🎧 01 Complete the questions with the words in the box. Then listen and check your answers.

help   mean   repeat   say   speak   ~~spell~~

1 Can you *spell* that?
2 Can you _____ more slowly?
3 How do you _____ that in English?
4 Can you _____ that, please?
5 What does that _____?
6 Can you _____ me?

B Complete the conversations with the questions from Exercise A.

1 A: My name is Elvira.
    B: _____
    A: Sure. It's E-L-V-I-R-A.
    B: Thank you.

2 A: Open your books to page 24.
    B: _____
    A: Yes. Open your books to page 24.

3 A: "Excellent"? _____
    B: It means "very good!"

4 A: Hi, my name's Hiroyoshi.
    B: _____
    A: My name is Hi … ro … yo … shi.

5 A: _____
    B: It's "birthday" in English.

6 A: I don't understand the homework.
    _____
    B: Yes, of course.

3 GRAMMAR: *be* — statements and *Yes/No* questions

A (Circle) the correct option to complete the sentences.

1 Carlos *is / am / are* from Mexico.
2 *Is / Are / Am* they college students?
3 Jim *isn't / aren't* from New York City.
4 *Is / Am / Are* they English students?
5 I *am / is / are* from Hong Kong.
6 Pôrto Alegre *is / are / am* a big city.

B Read the information. Complete the sentences.

student card

Name: Kate
Age: 19
City and country: Barrie, Canada
Studies: Business

student card

Name: Hiro
Age: 23
City and country: Nagoya, Japan
Studies: Business

student card

Name: Rafael
Age: 31
City and country: Recife, Brazil
Studies: Music

1 Hiro —————— 23 years old.
2 Kate —————— from Brazil.
3 **Rafael:** I —————— 31 years old.
4 **Kate and Hiro:** We —————— business students.
5 **Kate:** —————— Hiro from the UK?
  Rafael: No, he ——————.
6 **A:** —————— Hiro and Kate business students?
  B: Yes, they ——————
7 **Rafael:** —————— you from Canada?
  Kate: Yes, I ——————.
8 **Rafael:** —————— you music students?
  Kate and Hiro: No, we ——————.
9 **Hiro:** Is Kate 19?
  Rafael: Yes, she ——————.

WATCH OUT!

(X) She has 25 years.
(✓) ————————————————.

C Complete the conversation between Kate and Hiro. Use short forms where possible.

Kate: Hi. I **(1)** —————— Kate. I **(2)** —————— from Canada.
Hiro: My name **(3)** —————— Hiro. I **(4)** —————— from Nagoya.
It **(5)** —————— in Japan. **(6)** —————— you from Toronto?
Kate: No, I **(7)** —————— from Toronto. I **(8)** —————— from Barrie.
Hiro: **(9)** —————— it a big city?
Kate: No, it **(10)** ——————. It **(11)** —————— a small town.
(12) —————— you a business student?
Hiro: Yes, I **(13)** ——————. We **(14)** —————— in the same class!

A 🎧 02 Complete the conversation with the phrases in the box. Then listen and check your answers.

| Excuse me | please | Thanks | Thank you | You're welcome |

Receptionist: (1) _____, can you spell your last name, (2) _____?

Ms. Cardoza: Yes, it's C-A-R-D-O-Z-A.

Receptionist: (3) _____. And what's your phone number?

Ms. Cardoza: It's (555) 214-0091.

Receptionist: OK. You're in room 235. Here's your room key.

Ms. Cardoza: (4) _____.

Receptionist: (5) _____. Enjoy your stay.

B Look at the pictures. Complete the conversations with polite phrases from Exercise A.

5 VOCABULARY: ordinal numbers

A 🔊 03 Listen and write the ordinal numbers you hear. Write the numbers in the first column.

1	9ᵗʰ	ninth
2		
3		
4		
5		
6		

B Now write each number in words in the second column.

C Read the sentences. Write the words in bold as ordinal numbers.

1 This Saturday is the **twenty-seventh**.   _____
2 My next class is on Tuesday the **eleventh**.   _____
3 My birthday is on August the **thirteenth**.   _____
4 Today is September **twenty-second**.   _____
5 Independence Day in the U.S.A. is on July the **fourth**.   _____
6 The last day of June is the **thirtieth**.   _____

6 GRAMMAR: *be—wh-* questions

A Complete the questions with the correct question word in the box.

How	What	When	Where

1 _____ are you from?   3 _____ old are you?
2 _____ is your name?   4 _____ is your birthday?

B 🔊 04 Listen to the voicemail message and complete the form.

First name:	
Last name:	
Country:	
Age:	
Telephone number:	

C Complete the questions and answers about the woman from Exercise B. Use questions from Exercise A in the correct form.

1 **A:** _____ her first name?
   B: Her first name is _____.
2 **A:** _____
   B: Her last name is _____.
3 **A:** _____
   B: She's from _____.
4 **A:** _____
   B: She is _____ years old.
5 **A:** _____ her phone number?
   B: It's _____.

WATCH OUT!
(✗) Where you are from?
(✓)

Listen and write

A 🎧 **05** Listen to the conversation. Complete the online form with the information.

First name:

Last name:

Age:

Birthday:

Email:
kate192@mail.com

B Complete the form with your information.

First name:

Last name:

Age:

Birthday:

Email:

Over to You

C 🖊 Use the information in the form in Exercise B to write a paragraph about yourself.

My first name's …

WRITING TUTOR

My name is … / I'm …
My … is on …
My … is …

8

DOWN TIME

A Find the ordinal numbers in the wordsearch and write them below. The words can go forwards (→), down (↓), or diagonally(↗).

S	E	V	E	N	T	E	E	N	T	H
F	I	R	S	T	L	W	Y	N	V	F
S	C	T	M	N	X	Y	L	Q	H	T
F	E	H	N	D	D	D	X	T	T	N
O	T	V	R	G	N	B	N	E	W	T
U	F	M	E	O	V	E	C	N	P	P
R	L	I	C	N	E	W	L	T	K	D
T	B	E	F	T	T	J	Y	H	R	T
H	S	B	F	T	P	H	C	I	M	K
F	R	I	M	W	H	K	H	P	C	L
Q	F	J	K	K	F	T	B	N	N	L

5th   15th   1st   4th   2nd   17th   3rd   10th   7th

1 _____
2 _____
3 _____
4 _____
5 _____
6 _____
7 _____
8 _____
9 _____

B Complete the sentences with the missing word. Which are the letters in the circles?

1 Lucia ⃝ __ from Brazil.

2 August is the __ __ ⃝ __ __ __ month of the year.

3 Can you __ __ ⃝ __ __ more slowly?

4 Can you ⃝ __ __ __ me?

5 How __ ⃝ __ are you?

6 What does this __ __ __ ⃝ ?

7 Can you ⃝ __ __ __ __ that?

Letters in circles: 1 __ 2 __ 3 __ 4 __ 5 __ 6 __ 7 __

C Now unscramble the circled letters. What's the new word?

_____

UNIT 2 WHAT DO YOU DO?

1 VOCABULARY: occupations

A Unscramble the occupations and match them to the correct picture.

1 otrcdo _____
2 eirfifhegtr _____
3 atxi eridvr _____

4 nnergeie _____
5 ilcpeo rficofe _____
6 rtiwre _____

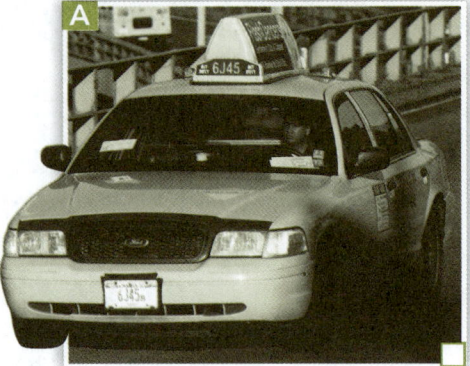
A

B

C

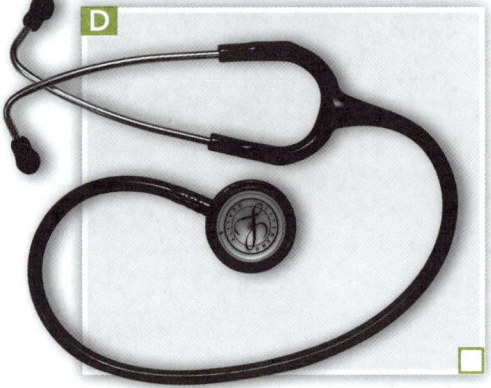
D

E

F

B 06 Listen to Teresa. What is her opinion about these occupations? Number the occupations, according to her opinion, from interesting (1) to not interesting (6).

☐ engineer
☐ police officer
☐ doctor

☐ firefighter
☐ writer
☐ taxi driver

2 GRAMMAR: articles

A Decide if the words use *a*, *an*, or no article (–). Write them in the table.

actor   artist   engineer   lawyers   musician   singer   students   teacher   writers

a	an	–

B Circle the correct option to complete the sentences.

1 My sister is *a* / *an* / *the* / – engineer.
2 Washington, D.C. is *a* / *an* / *the* / – capital of the U.S.A.
3 My brothers are *a* / *an* / *the* / – actors.
4 Our band is on *a* / *an* / *the* / – internet.
5 We're *a* / *an* / *the* / – actors on a TV show. *A* / *An* / *The* / – show is on Mondays.

C There is one mistake in each sentence. Rewrite the sentences correctly.

1 Are you teacher? _____
2 They are a doctors in a hospital. _____
3 My brother is a doctors. _____
4 Is Dave an lawyer? _____
5 I am not student. _____
6 My brother is teacher in a school. A school is in Boston _____

> **WATCH OUT!**
>
> ✗ He is musician.
> ✓ _____

3 VOCABULARY: family members

A 🎧 07 Listen to Marta describing her family.
Write the names in the box in the correct places.

| Bianca Clara Hector Juan Lisa Martin Rita Sasha |

1 _____

2 _____ 3 _____

4 _____ 5 _____ 6 _____ Marta

7 _____ 8 _____

B Use the family tree in Exercise A to complete the sentences.

Marta: Clara is my **(1)** _____ . Bianca and Hector are my
(2) _____ . Juan is my **(3)** _____ . Rita is
my **(4)** _____ . **(5)** _____ is her husband.
(6) _____ and **(7)** _____ are their daughters.
Bianca and Hector are their **(8)** _____ .

4 LISTENING: for specific information

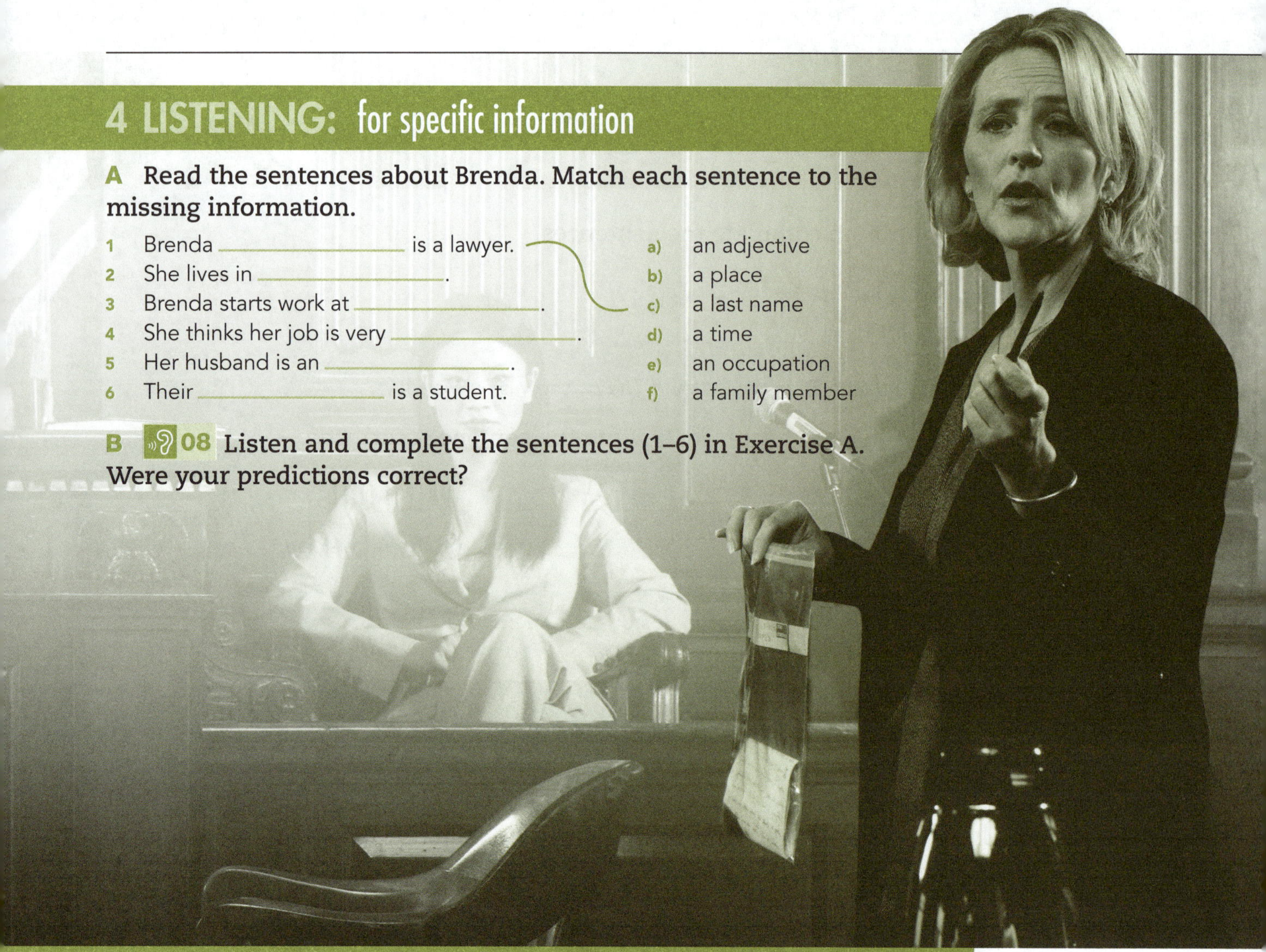

A Read the sentences about Brenda. Match each sentence to the missing information.

1   Brenda _____ is a lawyer.   a) an adjective
2   She lives in _____ .   b) a place
3   Brenda starts work at _____ .   c) a last name
4   She thinks her job is very _____ .   d) a time
5   Her husband is an _____ .   e) an occupation
6   Their _____ is a student.   f) a family member

B ») 08 Listen and complete the sentences (1–6) in Exercise A. Were your predictions correct?

5 GRAMMAR: possession

A Complete the sentences with the correct form of *have*. Use contractions.

Gina	✓ brother	✗ sister
Tom	✗ brother	✓ sister
Andy and Pete	✗ laptop	✓ bicycle
me	✓ laptop	✗ bicycle

1   Gina _____ a brother, but she _____ _____ a sister.
2   Tom _____ _____ a brother, but he _____ a sister.
3   Andy and Pete _____ _____ laptops, but they _____ bicycles.
4   I _____ a laptop, but I _____ _____ a bicycle.

B Complete the sentences with the possessive form of the words in parentheses.

1   Her _____ (*sister*) husband is a doctor.
2   Our _____ (*children*) teacher is from England.
3   _____ (*Tom*) parents live in Santiago.
4   My _____ (*mother*) best friend is from Argentina.
5   His _____ (*grandparents*) house is near the school.
6   Your _____ (*parents*) jobs are very exciting.

WATCH OUT!

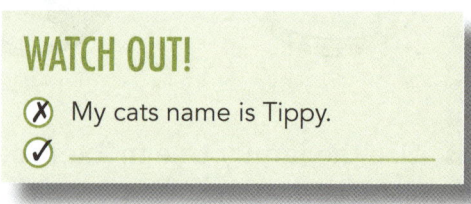

ⓧ My cats name is Tippy.
ⓥ _____

12

C Complete the sentences with the correct possessive pronoun.

1 Her name isn't Alexa. Alexa is my name. _____ name is Tania.
2 She doesn't have a red bicycle. I have a red bicycle. This bicycle is _____.
3 They live in a big house. This is their house. This house is _____.
4 Our classroom is 5A. Your classroom is 6B. Classroom 5A is _____, and classroom 6B is _____.
5 Rachel is a teacher, and Bob is a firefighter. Her job isn't dangerous, but _____ is very dangerous.
6 She has green eyes, and he has blue eyes. _____ eyes are green, and _____ eyes are blue.

6 WRITING: understanding the mechanics

A There is one mistake with capital letters in each of the sentences. Find the mistake and match it to a rule. Then correct the mistakes.

1 My birthday is in ꞥovember. _____   **a)** languages
2 We are from peru.   **b)** countries
3 They study english.   **c)** names of people
4 My sister and i are doctors.   **d)** towns, cities, and states
5 My teacher is Mr. daniels.   **e)** days of the week
6 it is five o'clock.   **f)** months
7 Antonia lives in texas.   **g)** the word *I*
8 Your class is on wednesday.   **h)** the beginning of a sentence

B Read the paragraph. Make six sentences. Add periods at the end of the sentences and capital letters at the beginning of the sentences.

my sister Alison is a writer she writes short stories and books for children her job is very interesting, but it is also difficult she sometimes travels around the country and talks about her work her books are very popular with children and adults she has two awards for best children's books of the year

1 _____
_____
2 _____
_____
3 _____
_____
4 _____
_____
5 _____
_____
6 _____
_____

Read and write

A Read about Max Garcia's life. What is his job?

Max Garcia is my cousin. He's 33, and he's a sound engineer. He's from the U.S., but he lives in London. He speaks French and Spanish (and English!). He loves his job because he listens to great bands from all over the world, and he meets famous musicians.

Max has a big family. His two brothers live in Miami, and his sister lives in Madrid. Max's dad, Alan, is a police officer, and his mom is a piano teacher. Max visits his family twice a year.

B Read the article again, and answer the questions.

1 How old is Max?

2 Is he happy about his job? Why?

3 Is Max's family small?

4 What's his dad's name?

5 What is his mom's job?

C Complete the table with Max's information. Then add information about a member of your family.

	Max	A member of your family
Name	Max Garcia	
Age	33	
Nationality		
Lives in		
Languages		
Job		
Opinion about job		
Family members		
Other information		

Over to You

D In your notebooks, write a paragraph about your family member. Use your notes in Exercise C and the text in Exercise A to help you.

WRITING TUTOR

(name) is my …
He/She is a/an …
He/She is from / lives in …
He/She loves/likes his/her job because …
He/She has a big/small family.

DOWN TIME

A Read the text about Emma's family. Answer the question and write the names of the people next to the correct picture.

Hi! I'm Emma. I have two brothers and a sister. My mom's name is Brenda, and my dad's Mike. My dad's dad is Edward, and his wife is Annette. My mom's dad is Richard and my mom's mom is Eleanor. My mom has a sister. Her name's Lauren. My sister's name is Susan, and her husband's name is Sam. They have two children, Sara and Sophie. I also have two brothers: Rick and Andrew. Rick is married to Clare. They have a daughter. Her name is Naomi. My other brother, Andrew, doesn't have kids. Oh, and my husband's name is Tim.

Who are Edward, Annette, Eleanor, and Richard? Emma's _____

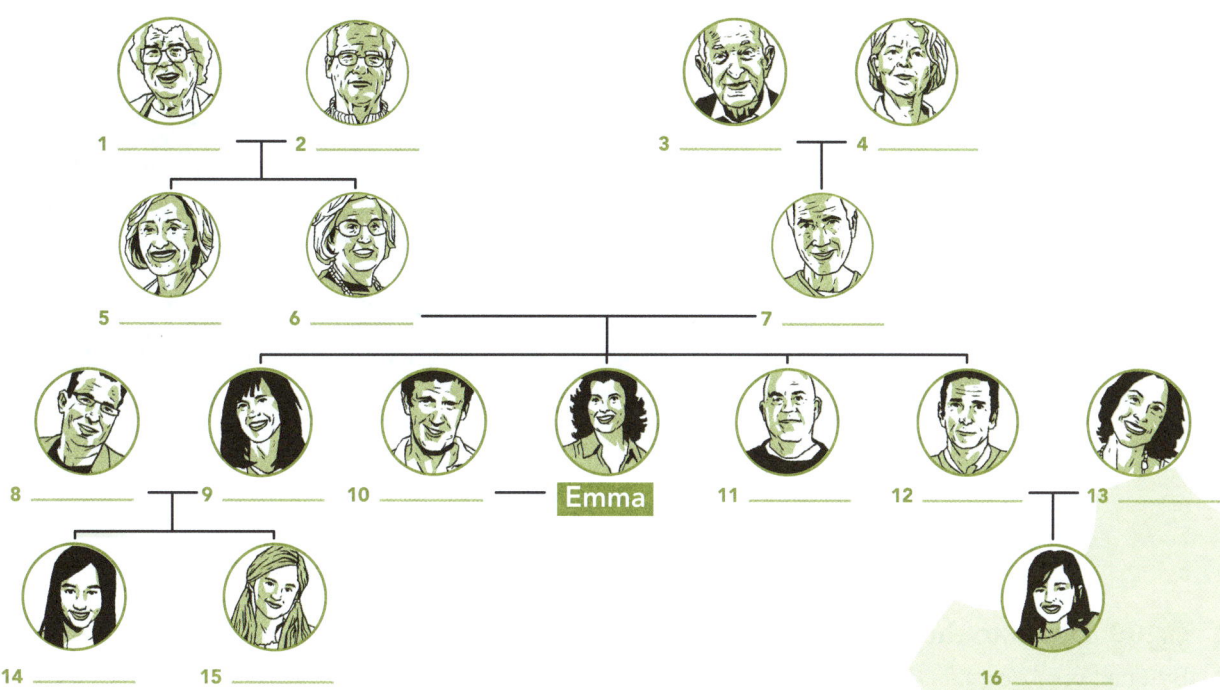

B Find the jobs. Separate the words with a line and write them underneath.

singersoftwareengineerlawyerartistfirefighterpoliceofficersoldiertaxidriverarchitectjournalistdoctor

_____

C Match the two halves to make words.

UNIT 3 DOWN TIME

1 GRAMMAR: simple present — statements and *Yes/No* questions

A Read the information about Rosina and Ken. Complete the sentences.

What do you do in your free time?

	Rosina	Ken
listen to music	✓	✓
read magazines	✗	✗
watch TV	✗	✓
play the guitar	✗	✓
buy CDs	✓	✓

Rosina

Ken

1 Ken _____ to music.
2 Rosina _____ TV, and
  she _____ magazines.
3 A: _____ Rosina _____ the guitar?
  B: _____, she _____.
4 A: _____ Rosina and Ken _____ CDs?
  B: _____, they _____.
5 A: _____ Ken _____ magazines?
  B: _____, he _____.

B 🎧 **09** Listen to the an interview, and ⟨circle⟩ the correct option.

1 Bettina *likes / doesn't like* country music.
2 She *plays / doesn't play* the guitar.
3 Bettina's parents *listen / don't listen* to music a lot.
4 She *buys / doesn't buy* MP3s online.

C 🎧 **09** Complete the interview. Listen again and check your answers.

A: Hi, Bettina. Can I ask you some questions for a survey?
B: Sure! Go ahead.
A: **(1)** _____ to music?
B: Yes, I do. I listen to country music. I really like country music.
A: And **(2)** _____ the guitar?
B: No, I don't.
A: **(3)** _____ to music a lot?
B: No, they don't.
A: **(4)** _____ a lot of CDs?
B: No, I don't. I **(5)** _____ MP3s online.
A: Great! That's all. Thanks a lot!
B: Sure, no problem.

WATCH OUT!

Does he read books?
✗ Yes, he reads.
✓ _____

2 READING: recognizing cognates

A Read the text, and circle the cognates.
These words will help you understand the text.

DO YOU LIKE TO READ BOOKS?

Share your opinions about your favorite books here.

I like mystery stories. I have a big collection of Agatha Christie books. I love puzzles, and I always try to find the solution before the end! Sherlock Holmes and Miss Marple are my favorite detectives. – Suzie

I like fantasy novels – especially when there is a series of books with the same characters. My favorite is *A Song of Ice and Fire*. I imagine I'm one of the people in the book! – Danni

I only read biographies and historical books. I want to read about real events and real people. I don't like fantasies or romantic novels. – Leo

I love a good romantic story. I can live in a fantasy world for a short time. And there is always a happy ending. – Monica

B Answer these questions about the text in Exercise A.

1 Who doesn't like fiction? _____
2 Who likes to live in a different world? _____ and _____
3 Who likes true stories about people? _____
4 Who likes love stories? _____
5 Who has a lot of books by the same author? _____ and _____

3 VOCABULARY: free-time activities

A Match the columns to make free-time activities.

1 play   a) TV
2 work   b) video games
3 listen to   c) friends
4 go   d) the movies
5 play   e) music
6 go to   f) bowling
7 see   g) out
8 watch   h) sports

B Complete the sentences with six of the phrases from Exercise A.

1 I often _____ with my friends in the evening. I love science-fiction movies.
2 Louisa likes to _____ on the weekend. She loves soccer and basketball.
3 I like to be in good shape, so I usually _____ at the gym twice a week. I use the weights and the treadmill.
4 We usually _____ on Saturday nights. It's not a difficult sport to play, and it's a good way to meet people.
5 Henry likes to _____ in the evening. He has a big collection of CDs.
6 John likes to _____ at night. He likes documentaries and game shows.

4 GRAMMAR: simple present—information questions

A Match the questions to the answers.

1 When do Bob and Jerry go bowling?
2 What do Jazmin and Paula do on Friday nights?
3 Where does Carmen usually play tennis?
4 Where do you do your homework?
5 Where does your brother buy music?
6 Who does Linda play tennis with?

a) Her sister.
b) In the park.
c) Online.
d) On the weekend.
e) They eat out.
f) At home.

B Read the survey about websites. Complete the questions with *What, Where, When, Why,* or *Who.* Then complete the survey.

Internet Survey

1 *What* websites do you visit every day?

_____

2 _____ do you like them?

_____

3 _____ do you visit them?

○ in the morning   ○ during the day   ○ at night

4 _____ do you talk about them with?

_____

5 _____ do you use the internet?

○ at home   ○ at work   ○ at school/college/university
○ in the library

WATCH OUT!

Ⓧ What she does in her free time?
✓ _____

C Read the text about Lisa. Then read the answers, and write the questions.

1 *What does Lisa like to do in her free time?* She plays tennis.
2 _____ With her friends from work.
3 _____ On Saturday mornings.
4 _____ In the park near her home.
5 _____ Because it's relaxing, healthy, and fun.

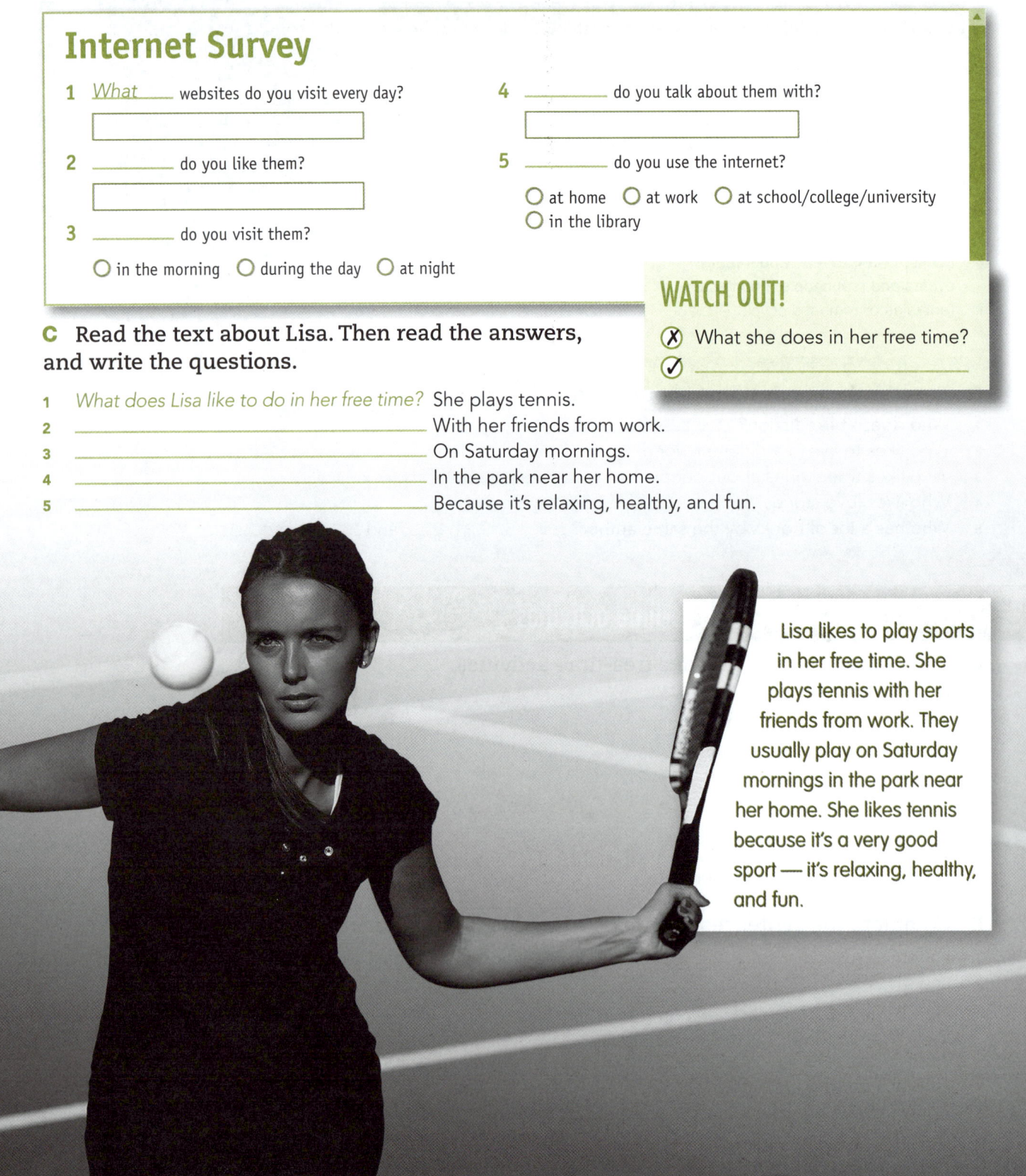

Lisa likes to play sports in her free time. She plays tennis with her friends from work. They usually play on Saturday mornings in the park near her home. She likes tennis because it's a very good sport — it's relaxing, healthy, and fun.

5 COMMUNICATION STRATEGY: asking for opinions

Complete the questions with the phrases in the box. Then match the questions to the best answer.

> Do you   How about   What do you   What's your

1   I don't like video games. They're too violent. _____ think?
2   I play soccer and tennis. _____ you?
3   I don't like classical music. _____ opinion?
4   This new science-fiction movie is great. _____ agree?

a)   I prefer hip-hop.
b)   Yes, I do.
c)   I don't play sports.
d)   I'm not sure. They're OK sometimes.

6 VOCABULARY: personality adjectives

A   »❿ 10 Listen and write the correct adjectives in the box under each picture.

> considerate   funny   loyal   popular   shy   sociable

1   Marisa: _____

2   Lucia: _____

3   Eddie: _____

4   Patrick: _____

5   Andrea: _____

6   Kyle: _____

B   Circle the correct option to complete the letter.

Dear Wendy,

I don't have many friends. I'm very **(1)** popular / shy. I sometimes go to parties, but I'm not very **(2)** confident / loyal, and I don't talk to anyone. My best friend is Amy. She has a lot of friends. She is very **(3)** independent / sociable and her stories are very **(4)** funny / considerate. She's an **(5)** introvert / extrovert. Amy introduces me to new people because she is a very **(6)** shy / loyal friend. But I'm an **(7)** extrovert / introvert, and I'm not **(8)** funny / shy. Please help me.

Sincerely,

Janet

Listen and write

A 🎧 **11** Listen to the radio show, and check (✓) the kinds of things the guests mention.

- ☐ their personality
- ☐ their free-time activities
- ☐ their daily activities
- ☐ their friends
- ☐ their family

B 🎧 **11** Listen to the radio show again, and write the person's initial next to the personality adjective. Write A (Alex) and J (Jenny).

1 shy _____   2 sociable _____   3 popular _____   4 funny _____

Then note the daily or free-time activity they like.

write new songs _____   watch a movie _____
go bowling _____   work out at the gym _____
see friends _____   practice the guitar _____
go to parties _____

C Read the short descriptions. Complete the text with the adjectives in the box.

> confident   funny   popular   sad   shy   sociable

a) My name's Lori. I'm **(1)** _____. I like going to parties and seeing my friends on weekends. I'm also **(2)** _____. I feel comfortable with new people and in new situations.

b) My name's Mark. I have a lot of friends and I am very **(3)** _____. I'm also **(4)** _____, and I like to tell jokes. I enjoy playing video games with my friends.

c) My name's Carla. I'm **(5)** _____ and quiet when I meet new people, but I have some very good friends. They are always there for me when I feel **(6)** _____.

Over to You

D Now make notes to complete the table with information about yourself. What are you like? What are your daily activities? What are your free-time activities?

Personality	Daily activities	Free-time activities

E ✏️ Now write three sentences about you. Write one sentence about your personality, one about your daily activities, and one about your free-time activities. Use your notes from Exercise D.

WRITING TUTOR

I'm very/quite …

I like/enjoy (going/playing, etc) …

DOWN TIME

A Write the phrases in the box under the correct pictures.

go bowling   go online   go to the movies   listen to music
play tennis   play video games   watch TV

1 _____

2 _____

3 _____

4 _____

5 _____

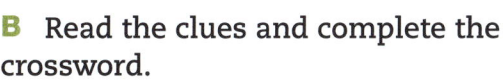

6 _____

7 _____

B Read the clues and complete the crossword.

1 Someone who tells jokes and is good at it is …
2 Someone who likes to meet new people is …
3 Someone who is not nervous is …
4 Someone who is nervous when they meet new people is …
5 Someone with a lot of friends is …
6 People you like and see in your free time are your …
7 People who like parties and talk a lot are …
8 People who listen rather than talk and like quiet evenings at home are …

UNIT 4 DAY IN, DAY OUT

1 VOCABULARY: telling time

A))) 12 **What time is it? Listen and draw the times on the clocks.**

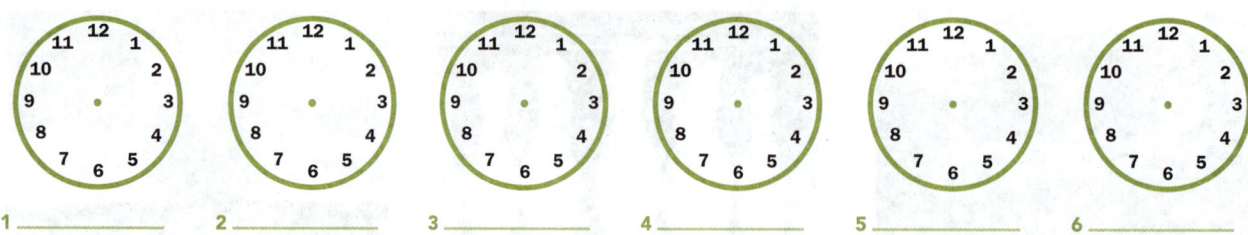

1 _____ 2 _____ 3 _____ 4 _____ 5 _____ 6 _____

B Write the time in words under each clock.

2 GRAMMAR: frequency adverbs and adverbial phrases

A Number the frequency words in order from high (100% = 1) to low (0% = 6).

☐ sometimes   ☐ often   ☐ rarely   ☐ usually   ☐ never   ☐ always

B Put the words in the correct order to form sentences.

1 always / at home / are / We / in the evening / .
_____

2 once a week / have dinner in a restaurant / Frank and Emilia / .
_____

3 Yolanda / watches / TV / rarely / .
_____

4 My brother / online / often / in the morning / is / .
_____

5 any free time / has / never / Hector / .
_____

6 three times a week / Clare / drives to work / .
_____

> **WATCH OUT!**
>
> ✗ He never is late.
> ✓ _____

C Rewrite the sentences with the correct frequency adverbs in the box.

| always (x 2)   never   often   rarely   sometimes   usually |

1 Suzanna takes the bus every day.
   Suzanna *always takes the bus*.
2 Frank and Liz go to the movies twice a week.
   Frank and Liz _____
3 Matt goes swimming every day on his lunch break.
   _____
4 Marie eats in a restaurant once a year.
   _____
5 We drive to work four times a week.
   _____
6 Leona is absent about once a month.
   _____
7 Toby doesn't get up early on Sundays.
   _____

3 LISTENING: for specific information

A 🎧 **13** Listen to Amanda describing her week. Match the days of the week to the activities.

1	Monday	**a)**	watch my brother's children
2	Tuesday	**b)**	go to the office
3	Wednesday	**c)**	go bowling
4	Thursday	**d)**	work out in the gym
5	Friday	**e)**	ride my bike
6	Saturday	**f)**	go shopping
7	Sunday	**g)**	go dancing

B 🎧 **14** Listen to Greg describing his week. <u>Underline</u> the mistakes in the text below.

Hi. My name is Greg. I'm an architect. On Mondays, I usually stay home and work on the computer. The rest of the week I work at home. I finish work at about 3 o'clock. On Tuesday nights, I stay home. On Wednesday nights, I have dinner with a friend. On Thursday nights, I usually go swimming. On Friday nights, I go to the movies. On Saturdays, I go dancing, and on Sundays, I go shopping.

C 🎧 **14** Listen again and correct the mistakes in Exercise B.

4 VOCABULARY: prepositions of time

A Complete the table with the words in the box.

> four o'clock   midnight   night   the afternoon   the evening
> the morning   the weekend   Wednesday   weekdays

on	at	in

B Complete the sentences with the correct preposition.

1 Ben usually goes shopping ⎯⎯⎯⎯⎯ Fridays.
2 I usually read the newspaper ⎯⎯⎯⎯⎯ the morning.
3 My favorite show starts ⎯⎯⎯⎯⎯ 6:00 p.m.
4 We sometimes watch TV ⎯⎯⎯⎯⎯ the evening.
5 Pete and Sally often go out ⎯⎯⎯⎯⎯ the weekend.
6 Pete goes to school ⎯⎯⎯⎯⎯ weekdays.

C Read about Mateo's daily routine. Put the events in the correct order on the timeline.

Mateo gets up at 6:00 a.m. He takes a shower before breakfast, and after breakfast, he reads the newspaper. He goes to work at 7:30 a.m. Mateo works until 12:30 p.m., and then he goes to the park for his lunch break. After lunch, he reads the newspaper again, and then he goes to the store to buy some food for his dinner. Then at 1:30 p.m., he goes back to the office. Mateo finishes work at six o'clock. After work, he goes home and has dinner. Before dinner, he watches the news on TV. After dinner, he reads a book and goes to bed at 10:30 p.m.

He gets up.

He eats breakfast.

He goes to work.

He goes to the park.

He goes back to the office.

He finishes work.

He has dinner.

He goes to bed.

5 GRAMMAR: clauses with *until, before, after*

A Read the sentences and check (✓) the sentences **a)** or **b)** that show the correct order of events.

1 Before she comes home from school, Bella plays tennis with her friends.
   a) ☐ First, she plays tennis. Second, she comes home.
   b) ☐ First, she comes home. Second, she plays tennis.
2 After we go to the gym, we have breakfast.
   a) ☐ First, we go to the gym. Second, we have breakfast.
   b) ☐ First, we have breakfast. Second, we go to the gym.
3 Antonio eats dinner before he goes home.
   a) ☐ First, he goes home. Second, he eats dinner.
   b) ☐ First, he eats dinner. Second, he goes home.
4 I go to the library after I go shopping.
   a) ☐ First, I go to the library. Second, I go shopping.
   b) ☐ First, I go shopping. Second, I go to the library.

B Join the two sentences. Use *before, after,* or *until.* Remember to use the correct punctuation.

1 We go shopping. Then we go to the movies.
   We _____. (*after*)
2 Danny goes to the library. Then he goes to his English class.
   Danny _____. (*before*)
3 My children watch TV. They stop when we have dinner.
   My _____. (*until*)
4 I practice the piano. I stop when it is eight o'clock.
   I _____. (*until*)
5 Zach and Mina cook dinner. Then they watch TV.
   After _____.
6 Becky goes to the gym. Then she has lunch.
   Before _____.

> **WATCH OUT!**
> ✗ He takes a shower after has breakfast.
> ✓ _____

6 WRITING: understanding the mechanics

A Read the sentences. <u>Underline</u> the subject and ⟨circle⟩ the verb in each sentence.

1 Toshihiko starts work at 7:30.
2 It is sunny and warm today.
3 Emil and Renata go to the gym on Saturdays.
4 My brother has a very interesting job. He is a travel writer.
5 We buy music online. We rarely buy CDs from a store.
6 It's five o'clock.

B Read the paragraph. The three words in the box are missing from the text. Put them in the correct places.

> goes   he   it

> Adam usually finishes work at 5:30 p.m. After work, goes to his English class. His class finishes at 7 p.m. Before he home, he goes to a coffee shop with his friends. Adam gets home at around 8:30 p.m. After dinner, he does his homework until is time to go to sleep.

Read and write

A Read this blog entry. <u>Underline</u> the frequency adverbs.

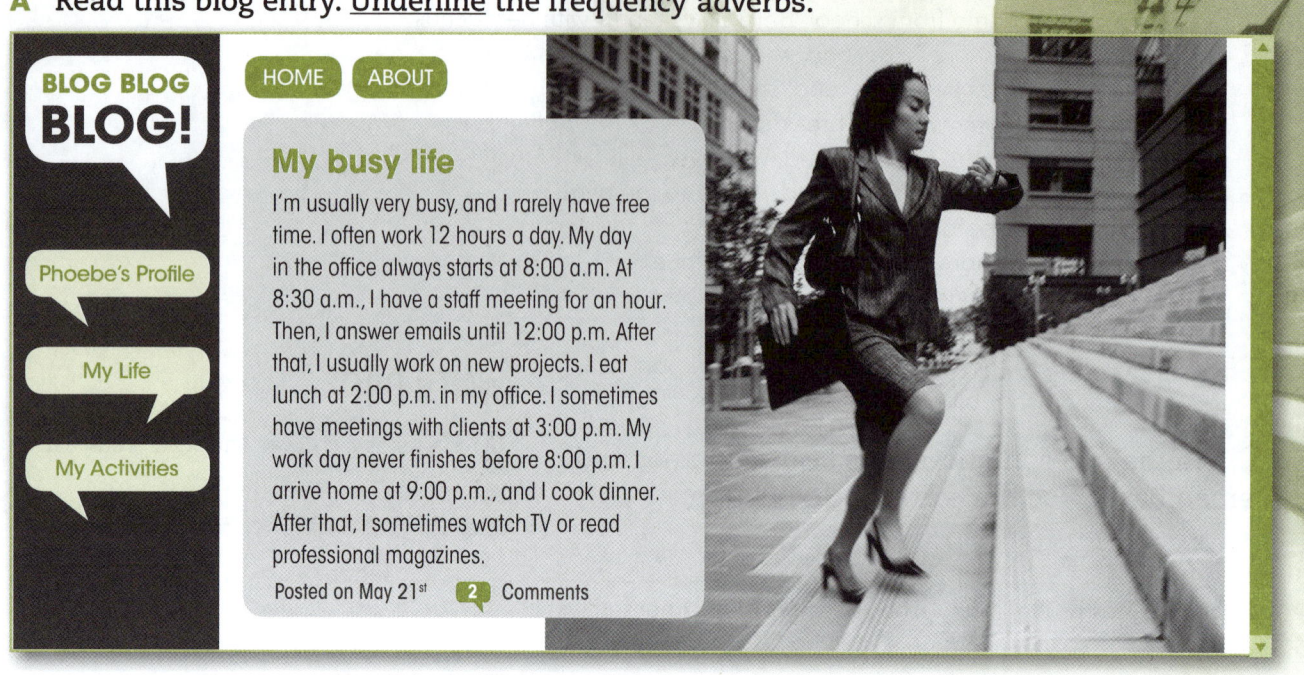

BLOG BLOG BLOG!

HOME · ABOUT

Phoebe's Profile

My Life

My Activities

My busy life

I'm usually very busy, and I rarely have free time. I often work 12 hours a day. My day in the office always starts at 8:00 a.m. At 8:30 a.m., I have a staff meeting for an hour. Then, I answer emails until 12:00 p.m. After that, I usually work on new projects. I eat lunch at 2:00 p.m. in my office. I sometimes have meetings with clients at 3:00 p.m. My work day never finishes before 8:00 p.m. I arrive home at 9:00 p.m., and I cook dinner. After that, I sometimes watch TV or read professional magazines.

Posted on May 21st   **2** Comments

B Make a list of the activities that Phoebe does during the day in the order they happen.

8:00 a.m. – Phoebe starts work.

8:30 a.m. –

Over to You

C Make a list of the activities you do during the day.

_____
_____
_____
_____
_____
_____
_____

D ✐ In your notebook, write a blog about your day, similar to the one in Exercise A. Use your list in Exercise C to help you. Remember to use frequency adverbs and sequence words to organize your ideas in a logical way.

WRITING TUTOR

I often/always/rarely …
I get up / go home at …
In the morning/afternoon/evening …
Then / After that, I …
At 12 p.m.
I … until 5:00 p.m.

DOWN TIME

A Read the clues and complete the crossword.

1 A … person is friendly and likes going out and meeting people.
2 a place to chat
3 every day
4 midday
5 not interesting
6 A … fan always watches and supports his team.
7 an earlier time
8 a form of exercise and sometimes I take my dog (three words)
9 article before a vowel
10 almost never

B Complete the sayings. Use the picture to help you. What word does each part of the picture represent?

1 Time waits _____ no _____.
2 Time _____ when you are having fun.
3 The early _____ catches the_____.

UNIT 5 HERE, THERE, AND EVERYWHERE!

1 GRAMMAR: *there is / there are* with *some, any, several, a lot of, many*

A Complete the paragraph. Use the affirmative or negative form of *be*.

Sydney, Australia is a fantastic place to visit for New Year. Every year there
(1) _____ a huge celebration on New Year's Eve. There (2) _____
a lot of events all over the city: music, fireworks, parades, picnics. There
(3) _____ a huge fireworks display near Sydney Harbor starting at
9 p.m. Arrive early because it's often difficult to find a good place to watch
the fireworks. Don't forget to book a hotel in advance because there
(4) _____ usually any hotel rooms left on New Year's Eve. About a
million people come to Sydney for New Year. There (5) _____ that
many cities that have a more exciting New Year's Eve party! Come to Sydney
and have a great New Year!

B Circle the correct option.

1   There *isn't / aren't* a lot of festivals in my hometown.
2   There *is / are* firework displays in the U.S.A. on July 4.
3   *Is / Are* there a big parade?
4   There aren't *some / many* music festivals here in December.
5   There aren't *any / some* tickets for the concert.
6   *Is / Are* there usually a lot of people at this festival?
7   There are *any / several* famous musicians in the concert.
8   There *is / are* a lot of visitors in the summer.

WATCH OUT!

✗   There is a lot of festivals.
✓   _____

2 VOCABULARY: places and attractions in a city

A Write each word in the box next to the correct definition.

art gallery   movie theater   museum   park   shopping mall   zoo

1   You watch movies here. _____
2   You see old and historic objects here. _____
3   You buy clothes and toys here. _____
4   You see paintings and pictures here. _____
5   You go for a walk here. _____
6   You see interesting animals here. _____

B 🎧 15 Listen and check (✓) the places the two friends plan to visit.

☐ art gallery   ☐ café
☐ movie theater   ☐ shopping mall
☐ park   ☐ museum
☐ zoo

28

C Write the names of the places in the box under each poster.

bus station   chocolate factory   movie theater   shopping mall

1 _____   2 _____   3 _____   4 _____

3 READING: for the main idea

A Read the three blog entries. Match each entry to its topic.

Blog 1	a)	a hotel
Blog 2	b)	a restaurant
Blog 3	c)	a park

B Is each blog in Exercise A positive or negative? Circle the correct option. Then underline the key words and phrases that helped you decide.

Blog 1: *positive* / *negative*
Blog 2: *positive* / *negative*
Blog 3: *positive* / *negative*

Tips for Tourists *Best places to stay at, eat at, and visit in Singapore*

HOME   FLIGHTS   HOTELS   RESTAURANTS   THINGS TO DO   ADVICE

1 Spend a day in **Gardens by the Bay** — it's awesome! There are beautiful rivers and lakes. There are amazing walking trails and thousands of varieties of flowers and trees, including huge "supertrees" — up to 50 meters high — with a walkway between them. It's an unforgettable experience.

2 **Raffles** is a must for any visitor to Singapore. Enjoy a taste of old-fashioned elegance and luxury. The rooms are large and comfortable with tall windows. There are several restaurants and tearooms — relax and enjoy a cool drink or drop by for a typical English afternoon tea.

3 Don't go to the **Singapore Grill**. There isn't any air conditioning. The waiters aren't helpful — the service is terrible. The food is cold and has no flavor. And it's too expensive.

4 GRAMMAR: the imperative

A Read the conversation. <u>Underline</u> all the imperative forms.

Rick: Excuse me. How do I get to the subway station?

Martina: Go straight ahead on this street for two blocks. Turn right on Fifth Avenue and go one block. Turn left on Ninth Street and walk for about 200 meters. Don't cross the street. The subway station is there on the left. Don't worry. It's easy to find!

Rick: Thank you very much.

Martina: You're welcome.

**B Complete the webpage with the words in the box.
Use the affirmative or negative imperative form.**

| drink eat forget give go have stay take visit walk |

New York City

I want to go to New York City for a weekend.
Please (1) _____ me some advice.

Posted at 07:53   Kathryn

Comments

(2) _____ the Metropolitan Museum and
(3) _____ coffee on the rooftop! There's a fantastic view!

Posted at 09:47   Lindsey

(4) _____ some New York pizza and
(5) _____ an ice cream soda — it's the best in the world!

Posted at 11:15   Emma

(6) _____ to buy a good guidebook. It's easy to get lost.

Posted at 11:41   Dale

(7) _____ in an expensive hotel. They aren't friendly.

Posted at 12:17   Jaime

(8) _____ a good street map. (9) _____
around Manhattan — it's fun!

Posted at 14:43   Duncan

(10) _____ to New York in the winter — it's too cold!

Posted at 15:15   Alan

WATCH OUT!

(X) Don't to forget your umbrella.

(✓) _____

C There is one mistake in each sentence. Rewrite the sentences correctly.

1 Don't to visit New York in the winter. _____
2 You go to some shows on Broadway. _____
3 Don't you take a taxi — they're expensive! _____
4 You buying some designer clothes and shoes. _____
5 Don't spending too much money! _____
6 Takes a ride around Central Park. _____

5 VOCABULARY: locations and directions

A Read the directions and mark the route on the map. Then complete the final sentence with your destination.

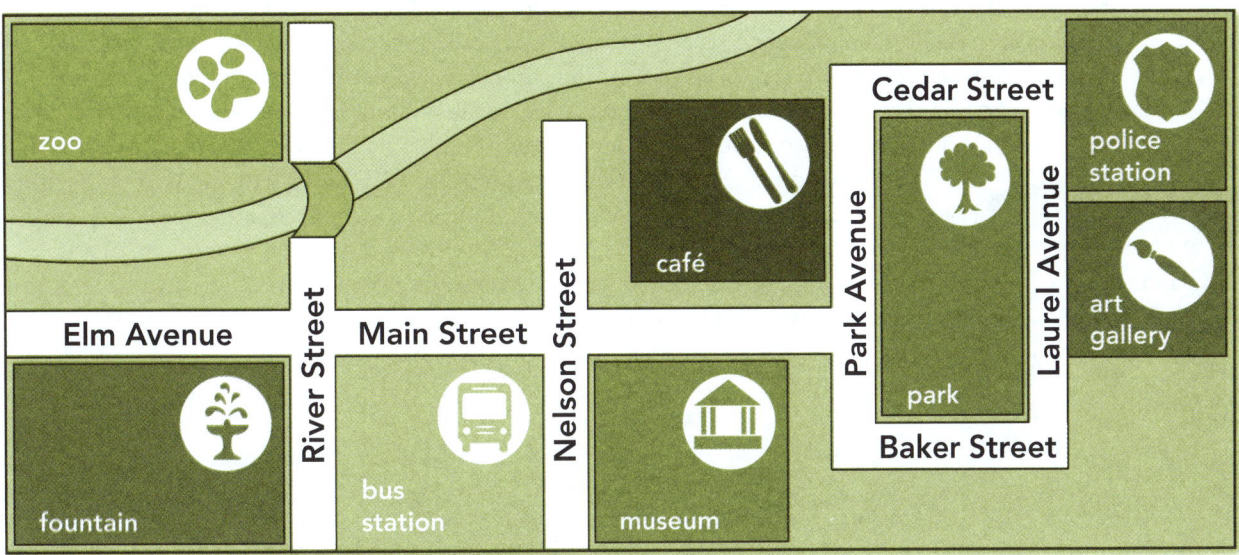

Start at the zoo on River Street. Go over the bridge and straight ahead. Turn left and go straight ahead. Take the second left and go straight ahead. Turn right and go to the end of the street. The _____ is on the corner of Cedar Street and Laurel Avenue, next to the art gallery.

B Look at the map in Exercise A again. Read the directions and write the places.

1 It's on the corner of River Street and Elm Avenue. _____
2 It's next to the police station. _____
3 It's between the museum and the fountain. _____
4 It's across from the art gallery. _____

C Look at the map in Exercise A again. Write the directions from the zoo to the café.

Start at the zoo …

_____
_____
_____
_____
_____

6 COMMUNICATION STRATEGY: repeating directions to check understanding

A Number the conversation in the correct order.

☐ **A:** Ah! First street on the right. OK, thanks.
☐ **B:** No, the first street on the right.
☐ **A:** Excuse me, how do I get to the library?
☐ **A:** Turn left. Then take the first street on the left.
☐ **B:** First, turn left here and then take the first street on the right.

B 🎧 16 Listen to the three conversations. Correct the directions.

1 You go straight ahead, and take the third left.
2 You take the first left. Then go straight ahead.
3 Go straight here, and then take the third right.

Listen and write

A 🎧 **17** **Listen to the short podcast about Edinburgh and complete the text.**

Edinburgh, the capital of Scotland, is an **(1)** _____ city. Stay in the old part of town and visit its beautiful **(2)** _____ and historical monuments. There are many castles in Scotland, but don't miss Edinburgh Castle because there you can learn about Scottish kings and queens, and see the crown jewels. At night, try the **(3)** _____. This way you can visit famous places from the *Harry Potter* movies. It starts at **(4)** _____ in the cemetery. Don't forget your camera, and bring warm clothes. In **(5)** _____ there is a famous international arts event. It's called the Edinburgh Festival. There are **(6)** _____, dance, music, and theater shows all day and night. Remember to **(7)** _____ early because there are over **(8)** _____ visitors during that month.

B **Read the text and complete these exercises.**

1 Circle the adjectives in the text. Which nouns do they describe?
2 Underline sentences in the text that give reasons. Which words or phrases introduce a reason?

Over to You

C **Choose a place of interest in your town or city. Then make notes about it using these points.**

- location
- adjectives to describe the place
- accommodations
- places to visit / reasons for visiting
- festivals / other information
- important tips

D ✏️ In your notebook, write a paragraph about the place you recommend to tourists. Use your notes in Exercise C and the text in Exercise A to help you. Remember to give reasons for your recommendations, and to use words and expressions to connect your ideas.

WRITING TUTOR

Don't forget/miss …
At night / In August …
There is / There are …
This way / … because …

DOWN TIME

A Look at these famous places and landmarks. Use the words in the box to complete the names.

Fountain   Museum   Park   ~~Square~~   Zoo

1   Red *Square* _____

2   San Diego _____

3   Trevi _____

4   Guggenheim _____

5   Central _____

B Find the cities for the famous places in Exercise A in the word search and write them. The words can go forwards (→), backwards (←), down (↓), or diagonally (↗).

H	E	R	P	E	T	H	E	B	O
N	R	E	A	A	N	D	I	G	E
E	M	O	R	V	R	L	E	E	R
W	Y	W	H	E	B	I	R	E	N
Y	B	K	Q	A	D	K	S	N	K
O	W	T	O	N	V	Z	L	F	M
R	T	L	A	H	L	F	Q	M	B
K	T	S	T	M	O	S	C	O	W

1 _____
2 _____
3 _____
4 _____
5 _____

UNIT 6 DIFFERENT STROKES

1 VOCABULARY: lifestyle adjectives

A  **18 Listen to these words that describe lifestyles. Write the words. Then check the spelling in your Student's Book or a dictionary.**

1 _____
2 _____
3 _____
4 _____
5 _____
6 _____

B **19 Listen to Emily talking about people in her family. Write a word from Exercise A to describe each person's lifestyle.**

Mom   Dad

1 _____   2 _____

Karen   Mark   Donna   Emily

3 _____ 4 _____ 5 _____ 6 _____

2 GRAMMAR: present progressive

A Write the -ing form of the verbs in the box in the correct column.

happen ~~have~~ live plan run study swim take talk wait win write

Add -*ing*	Drop *e* and add -*ing*	Double final consonant and add -*ing*
	having	

B Look at the picture and complete the sentences with the present progressive form of the verbs in the box.

drink eat listen read stand talk

1 Alice _____ a newspaper.
2 Martin and Emma _____ .
3 They _____ coffee.
4 Greg _____ to his MP3 player.
5 Ben _____ next to Alice.

C Write sentences to describe the differences in the pictures. Use the phrases in the box.

eat ice cream   feed the birds   have a picnic   listen to music
play the guitar   play with a dog   read a magazine   use a tablet

1

2

WATCH OUT!

Ⓧ The boy is play with a dog.

✓ _____

1 *In picture 1, the boy is playing with a dog, but in picture 2, he is eating ice cream.* (the boy)

2 _____ (the girl)

3 _____ (the man)

4 _____ (the woman)

5 _____ (the students)

3 LISTENING: for numerical information

A))) 20 Listen and write the numbers. Listen again and practice saying the sentences.

1 I'm _____ years old.

2 The time is _____.

3 My phone number is (_____) _____ - _____.

4 This building dates from _____.

5 My birth date is _____ / _____ / _____.

B))) 21 Leonardo Oliveira is calling the bank to check his credit card statement. Listen to Leonardo and complete his details.

Name: *Leonardo Oliveira* _____

Account number: _____

ID: _____

Amount on statement: $ _____

Problem: _____

Telephone number: _____

4 VOCABULARY: a green lifestyle

A Match the words to make phrases about being green.

1	buy		a)	trash
2	clean up		b)	water
3	reuse		c)	the lights
4	save		d)	a ride
5	share		e)	organic vegetables
6	turn off		f)	plastic bags

B Complete the sentences with words from Exercise A.

HOW TO BE GREEN

1 Don't throw away your plastic bags – _____ them.

2 Don't drive alone in your car – _____ a ride.

3 Don't leave trash everywhere – _____ it _____ .

4 Don't waste water – _____ water by fixing leaks.

5 Don't waste electricity – _____ the lights when you leave a room.

6 Don't use chemicals to grow food – buy _____ food.

5 GRAMMAR: present progressive vs. simple present

A Read the conversations. Circle the correct option to complete the sentences.

1 **A:** What *do you do* / *are you doing*?
   B: I'm an author. I *am writing* / *write* novels.

2 **A:** Where *does he go* / *is he going* right now?
   B: He *goes* / *is going* home.

3 **A:** What time *do they have* / *are they having* lunch every day?
   B: At 1 p.m. usually.

4 **A:** *Does she like* / *Is she liking* her new school?
   B: I *don't know* / *am not knowing*.

B There is one mistake in each sentence. Rewrite the sentences correctly.

1   I study now. I have an exam tomorrow.

   _____

2   Albert works very hard on his project. He needs to finish it today.

   _____

3   Raul is usually playing basketball three times a week. He wants to have a healthy lifestyle.

   _____

4   Kirsty isn't knowing Ben. They aren't friends.

   _____

WATCH OUT!

(X) I'm loving you.

(✓) _____

C Complete the conversation with the correct form of the verbs in parentheses.

Sue: Hi, Brad. What **(1)** _____ you _____ (do) these days?

Brad: I **(2)** _____ (study) at college right now. I **(3)** _____ (take) classes in computer science this semester.

Sue: **(4)** _____ you _____ (like) your classes?

Brad: Yes, they're fun! I **(5)** _____ (want) to be a video game designer when I finish. I **(6)** _____ (play) a lot of video games in my free time. Also, I **(7)** _____ (work) part time for a video game company right now. I **(8)** _____ (like) my job a lot!

Sue: That's great. Good luck!

6 WRITING: simple sentences

A Check (✓) the word that describes the underlined words and phrases in each sentence.

		Subject	Verb	Object
1	Joanna eats <u>organic food</u>.			
2	Ryan <u>recycles</u> bottles and jars.			
3	<u>Martha and Leo</u> waste a lot of water.			
4	I usually ride <u>a bike</u>.			
5	<u>Susanna</u> uses recycled paper.			
6	My sister <u>drives</u> an electric car.			

B Read the sentences. What kind of word is missing: subject, verb, or object?

1   *verb*   I often _____ to work.
2   _____ We usually recycle our _____ .
3   _____ Nowadays people are trying to save _____ .
4   _____ Some cars _____ too much gas.
5   _____ My _____ shares a ride to work with her co-worker.
6   _____ I always _____ the computer at night.

C Complete the sentences in Exercise B with the words in the box.

energy   neighbor   newspapers   turn off   use   walk

Read and write

A Read the text about World Environment Day. <u>Underline</u> the green activities.

World Environment Day is an annual event. Every year, countries all around the world organize activities to promote positive environmental action. Maria explains what people are doing in her city in Brazil.

"Today, my friends and I are planting trees in the park, and we're informing people about the ecological problems in the Amazon Rainforest. In the center of the city, people are riding bikes or using public transportation because today is also a 'No Car Day.' This morning, the local supermarket is only selling local food, and the Green Dream Team is cleaning up trash. I always save water, and recycle bottles and paper."

What are you doing to help?

B Now put a check (✓) next to the green activities you do.

- ☐ turn off the lights
- ☐ ride a bike to work/school
- ☐ buy local food
- ☐ share a ride
- ☐ use reusable bags
- ☐ take a shorter shower
- ☐ buy a reusable coffee cup
- ☐ collect rainwater
- ☐ do a cold clothes wash
- ☐ fix leaks

Over to You

C You are a reporter. You want to write a paragraph about what's happening in your town or city on World Environmental Day. But first plan and organize your ideas!

Think about:
- Introduction: What event? Why? Where? When?
- Development: What is happening? What do you do to help the environment?
- Ending: Short interesting sentence/question to finish.
- What time expressions can you use?

D ✏ In your notebook, write your paragraph.

WRITING TUTOR

Today, my family / friends / people in the city are …

I usually …

We also …

On weekends …

Today / Right now / Now / This morning …

DOWN TIME

A How green are you? How well informed are you about green issues? Take the quiz to find out. (Circle) your answers, and then check your results.

1 How do you travel to college or work?
   a) I take public transportation.
   b) I ride my bike or walk.
   c) I drive.
   d) I share a ride to work.

2 Do you reuse bags when you go shopping?
   a) I never reuse bags.
   b) I sometimes reuse bags.
   c) I often reuse bags.
   d) I always reuse bags.

3 How often do you buy organic food?
   a) I never buy organic food.
   b) I sometimes buy organic eggs at the supermarket.
   c) I grow organic vegetables.
   d) I usually buy organic foods.

4 Do you leave electrical items in sleep mode when you are not using them?
   a) I sometimes leave items in sleep mode.
   b) I never leave items in sleep mode.
   c) I often leave items in sleep mode.
   d) I always leave items in sleep mode.

5 What do people do on World Environment Day?
   a) take positive environmental action
   b) promote sustainable development
   c) discuss climate change
   d) all of the above

Now check your answers, and add up your scores.

	a	b	c	d
1	2	3	0	1
2	0	1	2	3
3	0	1	2	3
4	2	3	1	0
5	1	1	1	3

0–5 Your actions are damaging the environment! Find out what you can do to help!

6–11 Not too bad. You are environmentally aware, but you can do more to help the planet!

12+ You are a green star! You know a lot about green issues, and you are helping in many ways! Good job!

B Find the verbs in the word search to complete the phrases. The words can go forwards (→), backwards (←), down (↓), or diagonally (↗).

1 _____ water
2 _____ _____ the lights
3 _____ paper bags
4 _____ a ride
5 _____ public transportation
6 _____ _____ trash

C	S	E	L	P	I	O
T	L	P	E	K	A	T
U	S	E	M	T	A	E
R	A	C	A	A	S	V
N	V	K	R	N	O	N
O	E	U	S	E	U	O
F	J	P	O	C	A	P
F	S	H	A	R	E	U

UNIT 7 YOU HAVE TALENT!

1 VOCABULARY: personality adjectives

A Read the sentences and (circle) the correct option.

1 George always buys presents for his friends. He's very *optimistic / generous / honest*.
2 Everyone likes Patricia. She knows a lot of people. She's very *smart / patient / friendly*.
3 Yumi always makes a list before she goes shopping. She's very *organized / generous / optimistic*.
4 Steve feels angry when he has to wait for a long time. He's not very *reliable / friendly / patient*.
5 Fernanda always looks for problems in every situation. She's not very *smart / optimistic / honest*.
6 Elizabeth is a good friend. Her friends can depend on her for help. She's very *patient / reliable / organized*.
7 Denise always gets good grades in college. She's very *smart / friendly / honest*.
8 Stan is always truthful, and you can always believe him. He's very *patient / honest / generous*.

B Choose one adjective from Exercise A that describes you and one adjective that describes your best friend. Explain why.

I am optimistic because I never feel sad.

_____
_____

2 READING: for the main idea

A Look quickly at the text. What kind of text is it?

a) a personality test   **b)** an advice column   **c)** a horoscope

LIBRA September 23–October 22

(1) _____ You have no problems making friends this month. Your conversation and humor charm everyone.

(2) _____ Now is not the time to buy a new laptop. Only buy the things you really need.

(3) _____ You're stressed and tired. Drink herbal teas to get more energy.

(4) _____ You have an important decision to make about a co-worker. Be honest.

SCORPIO October 23–November 21

(5) _____ Be patient with relatives. Don't argue with people close to you.

(6) _____ This month is a good time to start your new diet. Go to the gym, eat fresh fruit and vegetables, ride your bike to work.

(7) _____ You want to move ahead, but there are many obstacles. Your boss knows that you are reliable, so don't worry.

(8) _____ Don't be too generous this month. You shouldn't spend too much.

B Read the text in Exercise A again. Write the headings in the correct place.

Family   Health (x 2)   Money (x 2)   Social life   Work (x 2)

3 GRAMMAR: *can/can't—ability*

A 🎧 **22 Listen and circle can or can't.**

1 Elena *can / can't* play the piano.
2 Peter *can / can't* dance.
3 I *can / can't* sing.
4 We *can / can't* drive.

B 🎧 **23 Listen and check (✓) the things that Ricky and Bella can do. Cross (✗) the things they can't do.**

	Ricky	Bella
play a sport		
speak another language		
cook		

WATCH OUT!

✗ Jeremy can speaks Korean.
✓ _____

C **Make sentences about Bella and Ricky. Use *can* and *can't*.**

1 Ricky / play tennis / .

  _____

2 Bella / play a sport / .

  _____

3 Bella and Ricky / speak another language / ?
  A: _____
  B: Yes, _____

4 Bella / cook / ?
  A: _____
  B: No, _____

5 Ricky / cook spaghetti / ?
  A: _____
  B: Yes, _____

D **Put the words in the correct order to form sentences and questions. Sometimes there is more than one correct answer.**

1 Marisa and Julia / speak / can / Italian / .

  _____

2 your brother / cook / Can / Indian food / ?

  _____

3 can / My best friend / sing / and / dance the tango / .

  _____

4 I / read music / play the piano / but / I / can / can't / .

  _____

5 she / play tennis / swim / can't / but / She / can / .

  _____

WATCH OUT!

✗ They can to play the guitar.
✓ _____

4 VOCABULARY: talents and abilities

A Write the phrases in the box in the correct column.

a car   chess   Chinese food   dinner   the guitar
the piano   to work   to school   traditional dishes

cook	*play*	*drive*

B 🎧 24 Listen and write each person's talents below.

Chloe

_____
_____
_____

Alicia

_____
_____
_____

Tony

_____
_____
_____

5 GRAMMAR: adverbs of manner

A Write the adverbs.

Adjective	Adverb	Adjective	Adverb
slow		good	
easy		bad	
beautiful		fast	
noisy		quiet	

B Rewrite the sentences with *can't* and the adverb form of the adjective in parentheses.

1   Sam swims, but he's very slow.
    He can't swim fast.   (fast)
2   Victoria speaks Japanese. She's a beginner.
    _____ (fluent)
3   Julia plays chess, but she's not very good.
    _____ (good)
4   Mike talks a lot. He is always very loud.
    _____ (quiet)
5   Robert reads books, but he's slow.
    _____ (quick)
6   My children ride bikes. They're slow riders.
    _____ (fast)

C What can these people do? Write a sentence about each picture. Use *can* and the adverb form of the adjective in parentheses.

WATCH OUT!

(X) She can very well play the piano.

(✓) _____

1   Pedro _____
    _____. (beautiful)
2   Kathy and Sally _____
    _____. (fast)
3   Francesca and Theo _____
    _____. (fluent)

6 COMMUNICATION STRATEGY: showing interest

A Read and choose the best answer.

1   Leona can speak five different languages.
    a) Wow, that's amazing!   **b)** Ah, that's nice.
2   Frank can cook excellent Thai food.
    a) Yeah? I can cook Indian food.   **b)** Really? I love Thai food.
3   Sam can play six musical instruments.
    a) That's good.   **b)** That's incredible!

B))25 Listen to each conversation. Check (✓) the conversations in which the first speaker shows interest.

Conversation 1 ☐
Conversation 2 ☐
Conversation 3 ☐

C))25 Listen again and practice saying the expressions for showing interest with the right intonation.

Listen and write

A 🔊 **26** Listen to each person's profile, and take notes on their personalities and talents.

Sara

2
He's _____ .
He can _____ .
He likes _____ .

Brianna

4
He's _____ .
He likes _____ .
He can _____ .

1
Sara loves _____ .
She's _____ .
She can _____ .
She's good at _____ .

Dominic

3
She's _____ .
She can _____ .
She likes _____ .

Dean

B Match the activities to the pictures.

1 do crosswords
2 take salsa classes
3 go to a dinner party
4 go bike riding
5 visit archeological sites
6 go to a karaoke evening
7 go to a concert
8 go fishing

A ☐  **B** ☐

C Choose suitable activities from the list in Exercise B for each person in Exercise A. In your notebook, write sentences to say why they like the activities.

Sara likes going to karaoke evenings because she enjoys singing.

C ☐  **D** ☐

E ☐  **F** ☐  **G** ☐  **H** ☐

Over to You

D Choose three adjectives to describe you. Then, in your notebook, write three things you like and are good at. Give reasons for your examples.

E ✏ Write a profile of yourself. Use your notes in Exercise D and the profiles in Exercise A to help you.

WRITING TUTOR

I'm …
I can …
I love …
I'm good at … / I'm not good at … + gerund

DOWN TIME

A **Play the word game. Follow these instructions.**

- You have five minutes to make as many words as possible from the letters in the grid.
- Each letter must be next to the next letter of the word it forms in the grid.
- Letters can be next to each other horizontally, vertically, or diagonally.
- Write your words in the space provided.
- Use a dictionary to check any new words.

_____
_____
_____
_____
_____
_____
_____
_____
_____
_____
_____
_____

B **Look at these words. Find the missing vowels and write the word.**

a e i o u

s m r t   _____

f s t   _____

f r n d l y   _____

h n s t   _____

p t n t   _____

r g n z d   _____

p t m s t c   _____

b t f l   _____

UNIT 8 SHOPPING AROUND

1 VOCABULARY: clothes

A What are Elena and Fabio wearing? Write the words for their clothes.

Elena

_____
_____
_____

_____

Fabio

_____
_____
_____

_____

B Make a list of the clothes you are wearing today.

_____
_____

2 GRAMMAR: *this, that, these, those*

A Complete the table with *this*, *that*, *these*, or *those*.

	T-shirt	Shorts	Jeans
Close to the person speaking			
Not close to the person speaking			

B Look at the picture. Complete the conversation. Use *this*, *that*, *these*, or *those*.

Yuko: Oh, I love
(1) _____ dress.
What a beautiful color!

Reina: Yes, (2) _____
color suits you. But what about (3) _____
skirts? You should try on
(4) _____ long one.

Yuko: Good idea. It's really nice.

Reina: What about
(5) _____ jeans for me? Should I try them on?

Yuko: Yes, try them on. And how about one of
(6) _____ sweaters, too?

Reina: OK. Where are the fitting rooms?

WATCH OUT!

✗ I like this jeans.
✓ _____

Reina   Yuko

3 LISTENING: for numerical information

A 〈🔊 27〉 Listen to the conversations and complete the table.

	Type of clothing	Price
1		
2		
3		
4		

B 〈🔊 28〉 Look at the pictures. How much do you think each item costs? Write your guess below the pictures. Then listen to the game show and write the correct answer on the label.

Your guess: _____   Your guess: _____   Your guess: _____

4 VOCABULARY: adjectives for describing gadgets

A 〈🔊 29〉 Listen and write the adjectives. Then check the spelling in your Student's Book or dictionary.

1 _____   3 _____   5 _____
2 _____   4 _____

B 〈🔊 30〉 Listen to the description of each gadget. Choose an adjective from Exercise A that describes it best.

1 _____   2 _____   3 _____   4 _____   5 _____

5 GRAMMAR: comparative adjectives

A Complete the table with the comparative form of each adjective.

Adjective	Comparative form	Adjective	Comparative form
small		popular	*more/less popular*
smart		exciting	
big		bad	
happy		good	
compact		pretty	
up-to-date		expensive	
cheap		easy	
old		slow	
attractive		high	

B Write sentences. Use the comparative form.

1 a game console / ↓ expensive / laptop / .
   A game console is less expensive than a laptop.

2 an MP3 player / ↑ up-to-date / a CD player / .

3 a digital camera / ↑ compact / a film camera / .

4 text messages / ↑ cheap / phone calls / .

5 my old computer / ↑ big / my new computer / .

6 desktop computers / ↑ powerful / laptops / .

7 my new smartphone / ↓ user-friendly / my old cell phone / .

8 my new office chair / ↓ comfortable / my old chair / .
   .

9 this e-reader / ↑ easy to use / that e-reader / .

10 his desk / ↑ small / yours / .

WATCH OUT!

(X) This computer is more better than that one.

(✓) _____

C There is one mistake in each sentence. Rewrite the sentences correctly.

1 An electronic dictionary is good than a book dictionary.

2 This camera is smaller my cell phone.

3 Our new TV is more larger than our old TV.

4 Phone calls on the internet are more cheap than by cell phone.

5 News on the internet is up-to-date than the newspaper.

6 My new computer faster than my old one.

7 My new tablet is user-friendly than my old one.

8 My laptop is more heavy than yours.

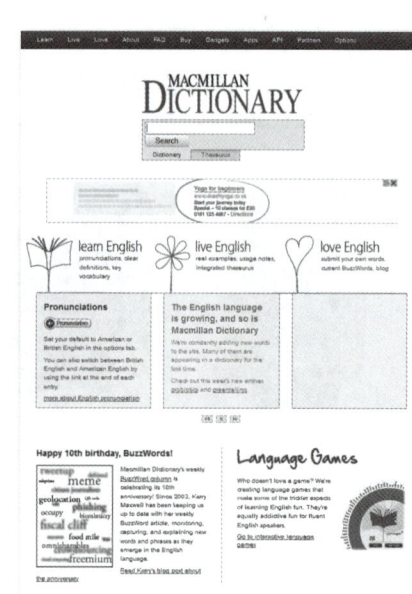

D Look at the pictures. Use adjectives from Exercise A to write correct sentences.

1 _____
2 _____
3 _____

6 WRITING: compound sentences

A Circle the best option.

1 These shoes are really small, *and* / *but* / *or* they aren't comfortable.
2 I want to buy a new laptop, *and* / *but* / *or* they're very expensive.
3 Do you want to buy this T-shirt now, *and* / *but* / *or* do you want to try it on first?
4 I like sending emails, *and* / *but* / *or* I prefer talking on the phone.
5 You can buy a computer here, *and* / *but* / *or* you can get one online.
6 This new MP3 player is more compact, *and* / *but* / *or* it isn't heavy.

B Choose the best ending to complete each sentence.

1 This new laptop is very versatile, and …
   a) it is powerful.
   b) it is too complicated.
2 My new computer is not compact, but …
   a) it is expensive.
   b) it is user-friendly.

3 You can call me, or …
   a) you can use the phone.
   b) you can send me a text message.
4 I like to buy clothes online, but …
   a) I sometimes get the wrong size.
   b) I sometimes save money.

Read and write

A Read about a new smartphone, and answer the questions.

HOME   PRODUCTS   REVIEWS   BUY   SEARCH

Are you looking for this year's best smartphone? Buy the R2 Sonic! It's very user-friendly and has a larger memory than the previous model. The bigger screen is good for pictures. Choose black or blue headphones. It has everything you need for a great price!

R2 Sonic
★★★☆☆

KAREN
★★☆☆☆
The R2 Sonic comes with blue headphones. They're cool, but heavy! There are a lot of games, but they aren't up to date.

PETER
★☆☆☆☆
I don't know about this phone. It holds 3,000 more songs, but I don't need 12,000 songs, and it's more expensive than the last model.

DIETER
★★★★☆
I love this phone. It's more compact than the previous model, but it has a bigger screen. It can store more pictures and songs, and the internet is faster because the memory is more powerful. I'd definitely recommend it!

1   Does Karen like the phone? Why or why not? _____
2   Why doesn't Peter like the phone? _____
3   What does Dieter like about the phone? _____

Over to You

B Choose a product to write a recommendation for. Write what you like and don't like about it.

Product: _____
Things I like: _____
_____
Things I don't like: _____
_____

C 🖋 In your notebook, write a product recommendation to post on a website. Use the ad in Exercise A and your ideas from Exercise B to help you. Remember to use *and*, *but*, and *or* to connect your ideas and write longer sentences.

WRITING TUTOR

It is ... and ...
I like ..., but ...
I don't like ... because ...
It comes with ...
You can choose a ... or a ...
I'd definitely recommend it!

DOWN TIME

A Find the 15 clothes items in the word search and write them below. The words can go forwards (→), down (↓), or diagonally (↗).

O	P	E	B	O	S	H	O	T	P	P	R	J
S	N	E	A	K	E	R	S	T	U	M	I	A
K	S	J	W	S	T	S	H	I	R	T	I	R
S	U	H	O	T	K	S	E	R	S	I	J	C
W	I	L	I	D	R	E	S	S	E	M	A	C
E	T	K	H	R	P	A	T	H	J	E	C	P
T	S	B	O	O	T	S	S	W	O	T	K	U
S	K	N	T	I	E	H	N	O	E	R	E	R
Y	I	K	I	R	T	O	O	P	A	N	T	S
C	R	D	V	U	J	E	A	N	S	U	I	S
K	T	T	R	S	H	S	W	E	A	T	E	R

1 _____ 4 _____ 7 _____ 10 _____ 13 _____
2 _____ 5 _____ 8 _____ 11 _____ 14 _____
3 _____ 6 _____ 9 _____ 12 _____ 15 _____

B Match the word parts to make adjectives and write them next to their definitions below.

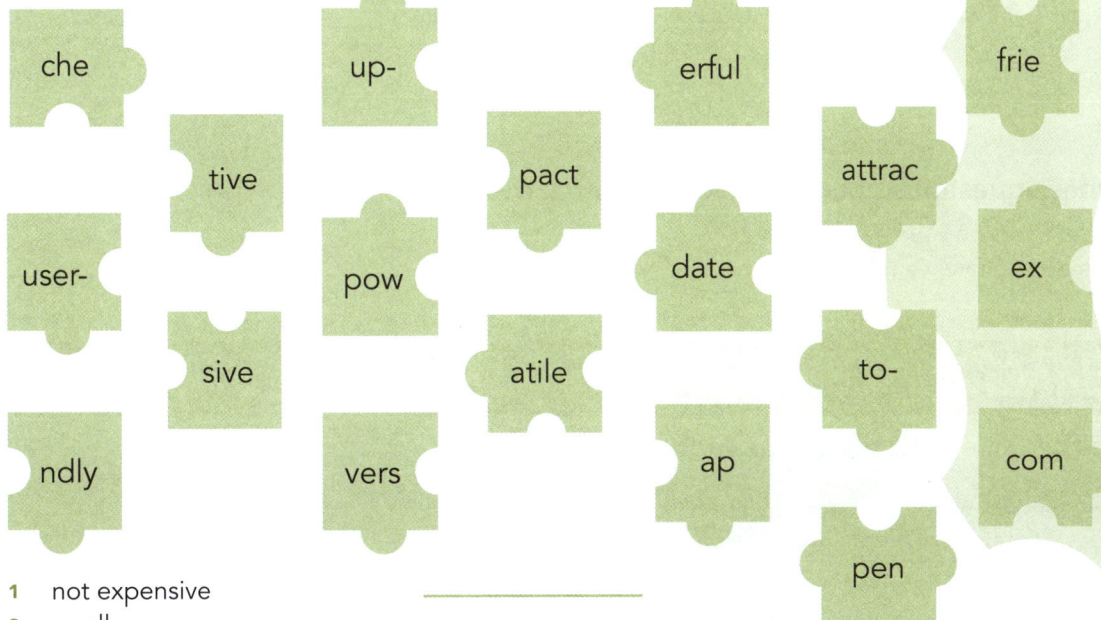

che · up- · erful · frie
tive · pact · attrac
user- · pow · date · ex
sive · atile · to-
ndly · vers · ap · com
pen

1 not expensive   _____
2 small   _____
3 stores a lot of information _____
4 easy-to-use   _____
5 looks nice   _____
6 can do different things _____
7 costs a lot of money   _____
8 modern   _____

UNIT 9 LET'S EAT!

1 VOCABULARY: food

A Label the pictures with the words in the box.

> bananas bread broccoli cheese
> chicken meat milk oranges peas
> potatoes rice watermelon yogurt

1 _____   2 _____   3 _____

4 _____   5 _____   6 _____   7 _____   8 _____

9 _____   10 _____   11 _____   12 _____   13 _____

B Put the words from Exercise A in the correct column.

Fruit	Vegetables	Grains	Protein	Dairy products

C Answer these questions about the food in Exercise A.

1 Which of these foods do you eat every day? _____

2 Which foods do you rarely eat? _____

2 GRAMMAR: count and noncount nouns with *some, any, much, many*

A Complete the table with the words in the box.

> apple banana bread butter cookies meat milk
> onions oranges potatoes tomato watermelon

Count nouns (singular)	Count nouns (plural)	Noncount nouns

B Complete the sentences. Use *a, an, much, many, some,* or *any*.

1 I'm really hungry. I want _____ big sandwich and _____ juice.
2 I want _____ cup of coffee, please. I don't want _____ milk – just a little.
3 Are you hungry? There aren't _____ cookies left – only two or three, but I think there is _____ bread.
4 There isn't _____ rice. Let's cook _____ pasta.

C There is one mistake in each sentence. Rewrite the sentences correctly.

1 I don't want an ice cream with my pie. _____
2 I don't want some vegetables. _____
3 I want any rice with my fish. _____
4 How much bananas do we have? _____
5 Do you have a bread? _____
6 Do you want cookie? _____

> **WATCH OUT!**
>
> (X) I don't drink many milk.
> (✓) _____

3 COMMUNICATION STRATEGY: using phone language

A Number the conversation in the correct order. Then ⬭circle the correct option.

☐ It's Alice, and my number is 568-4312. Thanks!
☐ Hi. Is Janice there?
☐ I'm sorry. She's out. Can I take a message?
☐ No problem.
☐ Yes, please. Can you ask her to call me tonight? It's important.
☐ Sure. What's your name?

The conversation is *formal* / *informal*.

B 》31 Complete the conversation with the phrases in the box. Then listen and check your answers.

Could I	Could you	isn't here	Thank you	Would you

A: Good afternoon. **(1)** _____ speak to Mr. Brown, please?
B: I'm sorry. He **(2)** _____ right now. **(3)** _____ like to leave a message?
A: Yes, please. **(4)** _____ ask him to call me back? My name's Mike Vodel, and my number is 460-0131.
B: Yes, of course.
A: **(5)** _____ .
B: You're welcome.

C Write a conversation like the one in Exercise B. Use the information in the phone message.

> **While you were out**
>
> Message for: Helen Stevens
> Message taken by: Lily
> Caller: Fred Stevens
> Message: Call him back at 450-3232

Fred: *Good afternoon.* _____
Lily: _____
_____
Fred: _____
_____
Lily: _____
Fred: _____
Lily: _____

4 GRAMMAR: verb phrases

A Circle the correct words to complete the conversation.

A: Would you **(1)** *need* / *like* to eat pizza tonight?

B: Sorry! I have **(2)** *study* / *to study* for my math test. How about tomorrow night?

A: OK! I **(3)** *want* / *like* to try the new pizza restaurant on the corner.

B: Good idea! I'd love **(4)** *go* / *to go* there. What time do you want **(5)** *meet* / *to meet*?

A: I **(6)** *need* / *like* to go the gym first, so how about 6 p.m.?

B: Let's **(7)** *make* / *to make* it 6:30, OK? I have **(8)** *take* / *to take* some books back to the library first.

A: Sure! See you later.

WATCH OUT!

Ⓧ Let's to go to the movies tonight.

✓ _____

B Match to make complete sentences.

1	Would you …	**a)**	to book a table for lunch, only for dinner.
2	Do you …	**b)**	to buy some tomatoes for the soup.
3	Let's …	**c)**	go for pizza on Saturday.
4	You don't have …	**d)**	like to go out for lunch tomorrow?
5	I need …	**e)**	want to eat Indian food tonight?

5 VOCABULARY: ordering in a restaurant

A Match to complete the phrases.

1	green	**a)**	cocktail
2	fried	**b)**	salad
3	shrimp	**c)**	soup
4	vegetable	**d)**	fish

B Label the pictures with a phrase from Exercise A.

1 _____ 2 _____ 3 _____

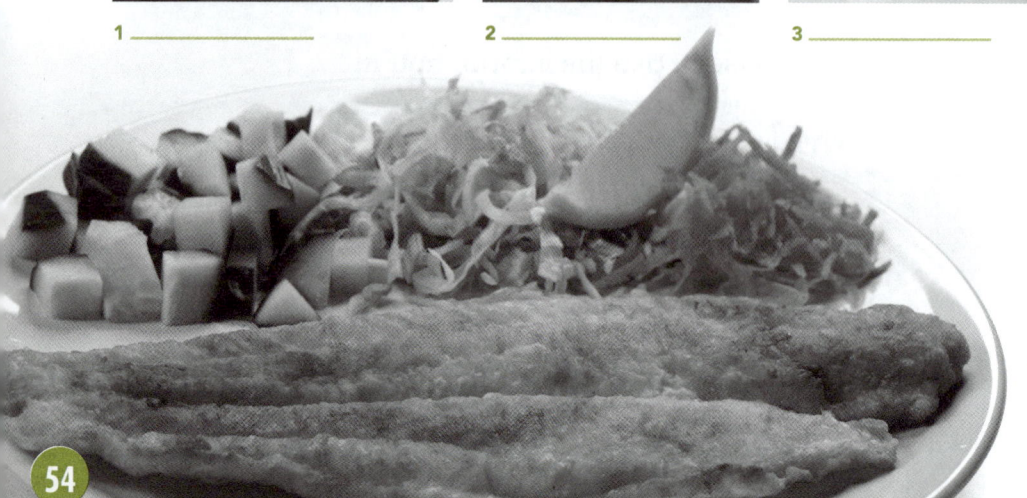

4 _____

C Look at the menu. Write the words in the box in the correct place.

Appetizers   Beverages   Desserts   Main courses

MENU

1 _____
mushroom soup	$3.99
shrimp salad	$4.99
spinach and cheese pie	$5.50

2 _____
fried fish and potatoes	$16.50
chicken salad	$12.50
spaghetti with meatballs	$15.50

3 _____
apple pie with ice cream	$3.99
cheesecake	$4.99
ice cream (strawberry, chocolate, or vanilla)	$2.50

4 _____
juice, soda	$2.99
coffee, tea (hot or iced)	$2.50

D 🎧 **32** Listen to Jessica and Brian ordering from the menu. On the menu, circle what Jessica wants to eat. Underline what Brian wants to eat.

E How much does Jessica need to pay, and how much does Brian need to pay? What is the total cost of their order?

Jessica's order: _____
Brian's order: _____
Total: _____

6 READING: scanning for specific information

A Choose the best menu for each person.
1 ☐ Daniela loves fish. She doesn't like cake or pies. She prefers fruit.
2 ☐ Susanna is a vegetarian, and she loves ice cream.
3 ☐ Michael is on a diet. He doesn't want to eat fried food or grains.
4 ☐ Bill doesn't like red meat, but he eats chicken and fish. He loves chocolate.

MENU 1

APPETIZER:
Vegetable soup
✻
MAIN COURSE:
Baked vegetables
with cheese
✻
DESSERT:
Cherry pie and ice cream

MENU 2

APPETIZER:
Green salad
✻
MAIN COURSE:
Baked chicken
✻
DESSERT:
Strawberries

MENU 3

APPETIZER:
Mushrooms and
garlic sauce
✻
MAIN COURSE:
Fried fish with rice
✻
DESSERT:
Ice cream and fruit salad

MENU 4

APPETIZER:
Shrimp cocktail
✻
MAIN COURSE:
Seafood pasta and
fried zucchini
✻
DESSERT:
Chocolate cake

B Which menu in Exercise A is your favorite? Why?

My favorite menu is Menu _____ because _____.

Listen and write

A 🎧 **33** Listen to the radio show. Circle the ingredients you need to make the recipe.

spinach   butter
bread   oil
strawberries   melon
nuts   vinegar
broccoli   salt
potatoes   paprika
cream   onion

B 🎧 **33** Listen again and number the instructions in the correct order.

☐ Cook for about one minute.

☐ Add the nuts.

☐ Pour this over the salad.

☐ Combine the oil, vinegar, paprika, and onion.

☐ Put the spinach, strawberries, and nuts in a bowl.

☐ Melt the butter over medium heat.

Over to You

C ✏️ Choose a recipe you like and know how to prepare. In your notebook, write the recipe, giving the list of ingredients and the instructions.

DOWN TIME

A Read the clues and complete the crossword.

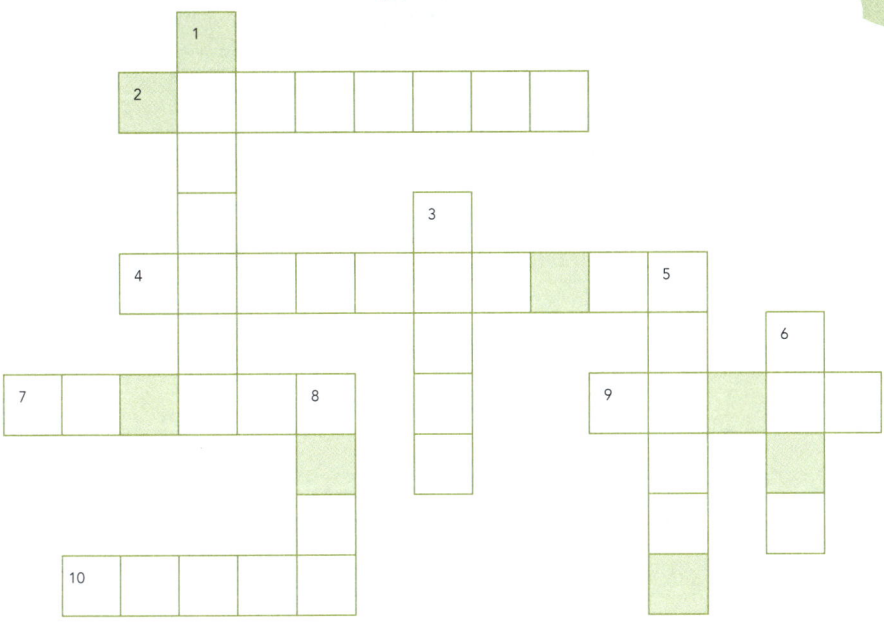

1 Meat and beans are … They give you energy.
2 Cheese and milk are dairy …
3 … chicken is made in the oven, not fried.
4 Make sure you eat lots of fruit and …
5 Jumbo fried … is a delicious seafood dish.
6 … is a type of red meat.
7 Soda and juice are types of soft …
8 Too much … is bad for your health.
9 … salad is made with lettuce and other green vegetables.
10 Apples, pears, and bananas are types of …

B Read the ingredients for the dish, and guess what the recipe is for. Write the name of the dish. Unscramble the shaded letters in the crossword to check your answer.

Recipe for: _ _ _ _ _ _ _ _

For the pastry:
2½ cups flour
½ teaspoon salt
8 tablespoons butter
6 tablespoons cold water

For the filling:
5 apples (cut into small pieces)
1 large lemon, juiced
1 cup dark brown sugar
1½ tablespoons flour
¼ teaspoon cinnamon
2 teaspoons milk

UNIT 10 SPEAKING OF THE PAST

1 GRAMMAR: simple past—affirmative statements

A Complete the table with the simple past forms of verbs in the box.

carry   decide   explain   like   live   marry   play   prepare   stay   study   try   watch

Regular simple past verbs

Add *-ed*	Add *-d*	Change *y* to *i* and add *-ed*

B Complete the table.

Irregular simple past verbs

Base form	Simple past form	Base form	Simple past form
do		meet	
know			spoke
	went		was/were
give		read	
	got		told

C Complete the paragraph with the simple past form of verbs in the box.

be   eat   go   have   see   stay   swim   take

WATCH OUT!

☒ I writed you a postcard last week.

☑ _____

Looking for vacation ideas?

Share experiences and get ideas for fun vacations here!

We (1) _____ to Hawaii on our last vacation. It (2) _____ amazing! We (3) _____ in a beautiful hotel near the beach. We (4) _____ in the ocean, and we (5) _____ a volcano. We (6) _____ a lot of pictures of whales and dolphins. And we (7) _____ some fabulous seafood. We (8) _____ a wonderful time and recommend Hawaii to anyone who loves beach vacations.

SUBMIT COMMENT

2 VOCABULARY: adjectives with -ed and -ing

A Circle the correct option.

1 It's my birthday party tomorrow. I'm really *exciting* / *excited* about it.
2 We watched a terrible movie on TV last night. It was very *boring* / *bored*.
3 Tanya worked on this homework all night, and today she's just so *tiring* / *tired*.
4 I'm reading a great book right now. It's *amazing* / *amazed*.
5 I love playing basketball, but my friends aren't *interesting* / *interested* in sports.

B Complete the two sentences for each picture. Use an adjective from Exercise A with -ed or -ing.

Marta

Francisco

Diana

1 Marta's job is _____.
By the end of the day she's really _____.

2 The soccer game is very _____. Francisco is _____ about the soccer game.

3 Diana's new boyfriend is really _____. She listened to him for an hour, and she was so _____.

3 GRAMMAR: simple past—questions and negative statements

A Complete the questions and answers about Cathy's and Bill's weekend. Use the information in the table.

	Cathy	Bill
ate out	✓	✗
cooked dinner at home	✗	✓
met friends	✓	✓
watched TV	✗	✗

1 A: _____ Cathy _____ out?
  B: Yes, _____.
2 A: _____ Bill _____ out?
  B: No, _____.
3 A: _____ Cathy and Bill _____ friends?
  B: Yes, _____.
4 A: _____ Cathy and Bill _____ TV?
  B: No, _____.

5 A: What _____ Cathy _____ on the weekend?
  B: She _____ dinner at home. She ate out and met friends.
6 A: What _____ Bill _____ on the weekend?
  B: He _____ out. He cooked dinner at home and met friends.

B 🎧 **34 Complete the questions. Then listen and check your answers.**

1 _____ did you do on Friday night?
2 _____ did you go?
3 _____ you have a good time?
4 _____ did you go with?
5 _____ was the food?
6 _____ it very expensive?

WATCH OUT!

✗ What they did on the weekend?

✓ _____

C 🎧 **34 Match the answers to the questions in Exercise B. Listen again to check.**

a) ☐ Oh, fantastic. I love Thai food.
b) ☐ Yes, it was great.
c) ☐ I went out for dinner.

d) ☐ With my girlfriend.
e) ☐ Not too bad.
f) ☐ To the new Thai restaurant. It's fantastic.

4 LISTENING: understanding the main idea

A 🎧 **35 Listen to these conversations. Circle the main topic of each one.**

1 a) an exam   b) a vacation   c) an accident
2 a) a business meeting b) a vacation   c) an exam
3 a) a soccer game   b) a vacation   c) a celebration

B 🎧 **35 Listen again. Is each conversation about a positive or a negative experience? Circle the correct option.**

1 *positive / negative*
2 *positive / negative*
3 *positive / negative*

C 🎧 **35 Listen again and write any key words that helped you identify the main idea in each conversation.**

1 _____
2 _____
3 _____

5 WRITING: sequencing and connecting ideas

A Number the pictures in the correct order to make a story about Frank.

B Write Frank's story. Use connecting words: *first, then, after that, finally.*

*Yesterday morning, Frank was on his way to meet some friends
when he found …*

_____

_____

_____

6 VOCABULARY: memorable experiences

A Complete the sentences with the simple past form of the verbs
in the box.

get (x 2)   see (x 2)   take (x 2)

1   Martine _____ a famous person at the airport.
2   Frank _____ a pictures of Alicia Keys at a concert.
3   Emma _____ a fantastic gift from her parents – a new camera!
4   We _____ an amazing concert last weekend.
5   Rick _____ a special letter from his favorite movie star.
6   Miranda _____ a trip to Las Vegas for her birthday.

B Match the sentences to make conversations.

1   I saw an amazing concert last night.   a)   Wow! Who was it?
2   I got a special letter in the mail yesterday. b)   That sounds good. Was it interesting?
3   I saw a famous movie star in the shopping mall. c)   Oh, yes? Can I see them?
4   I got a birthday gift from my boyfriend.   d)   That sounds exciting. Who was it from?
5   I saw a movie about whales on TV last night.   e)   Really? Who was the band?
6   I took some pictures of all my classmates.   f)   Oh, yeah? What did you get?

Read and write

A Read this blog entry about Maria's experience. Look at the underlined words in the text. Match them to their function.

> I can't believe it! Last night I went out with some friends. We were in the restaurant when suddenly I saw the most gorgeous man ♥!
>
> It felt like I knew him, but I wasn't sure at first. <u>Then</u>, suddenly, I realized – of course I knew him! He is the singer of my favorite band. I love their music, <u>and</u> I love him, too! I was really excited and nervous …
>
> My friends told me to go and say hi, <u>so</u> I got up and walked over to his table. When I got there, I was so nervous that I hit the table and spilled his drink. I was really embarrassed, <u>but</u> he was very nice and didn't mind. <u>After that</u>, I asked him for his autograph.
>
> He was so amazing. Now I love him more than ever! ☺
>
> Maria

Contrast: _____   Consequence: _____
Addition: _____   Sequence: _____ _____

B Now read the text again, and put the events in chronological order.
- ☐ Maria felt anxious.
- ☐ Maria went out with friends.
- ☐ Maria recognized the man.
- ☐ Maria's friends said something to her.
- ☐ The man gave something to Maria.
- ☐ Maria had a small accident.

C Complete the questions that Maria's friend Annie asks about her experience. Then complete Maria's answers.

Annie: Where (1) _____ you go?
Maria: (2) _____
Annie: (3) _____ did you go with?
Maria: (4) _____
Annie: (5) _____ happened?
Maria: (6) _____
_____
Annie: (7) _____ did you feel?
Maria: (8) _____

Over to You

D Think about a memorable event that happened to you. Use key words only to answer Annie's questions in Exercise C about your memory.

1 _____
2 _____
3 _____
4 _____

E ✏ Now use the blog entry in Exercise A and your notes in Exercise D to help you write about your memorable event. Remember to use linking words to connect and organize your text.

WRITING TUTOR

I was …
I went …
It felt …
Then / After that ….
I jumped when the phone rang.
Suddenly …
Now …

DOWN TIME

A Complete the crossword with the simple past form of these verbs. Time yourself!

1 see
2 watch
3 like
4 be
5 carry
6 listen
7 put
8 eat
9 find
10 practice
11 meet
12 try
13 return

B Where did the girl go? The letters in shaded boxes spell the words for the answer.

_____

C Circle the phrases that are INCORRECT.

1 **a)** an amazing hotel
   b) an amazed hotel
   c) a boring hotel
2 **a)** take a vacation
   b) take a new hobby
   c) take a trip
3 **a)** a tiring trip
   b) a tired man
   c) an interested book
4 **a)** see a concert
   b) see a picture
   c) see a trip
5 **a)** take a picture
   b) make a picture
   c) take a tour
6 **a)** I'm tiring after the trip.
   b) I'm tired after the trip.
   c) I'm excited after the trip.

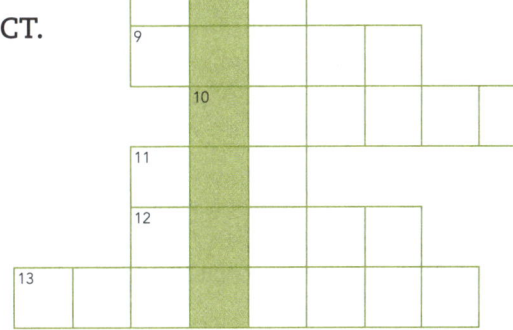

UNIT 11 GREAT LIVES

1 READING: scanning for specific information

A Scan the descriptions to find the answers to the questions below. The answer may be more than one person.

Aung San Suu Kyi

Marco Polo

Juliana Rotich

Aung San Suu Kyi is the leader of the democratic party in Burma. She won the Nobel Peace Prize in 1991. She became a member of the Burmese Parliament in 2012 after many years under house arrest. She fights every day for the rights of Burmese people.

Chico Mendes was an environmentalist who fought against deforestation in Brazil. He died in 1988 trying to save the Amazon from destruction.

Marco Polo was a Venetian explorer who was born around 1254. He explored distant countries like India and China. He learned many languages and wrote descriptions of everything he saw.

Jane Goodall was born in England in 1934. She is a naturalist who studied the life patterns of chimpanzees. She works in Tanzania to protect the chimpanzees and to educate children about her work.

Juliana Rotich was born and grew up in Kenya and later studied Information Technology (IT) in the U.S.A. She started a website called *Ushahidi* (meaning "testimony" in Swahili) to report violence around the world. She also fights to protect forests in Africa.

Stephen Hawking is a British scientist and author. Despite suffering from the debilitating illness Amyotrophic Lateral Sclerosis (ALS), his work in physics and cosmology is groundbreaking, and he wrote the bestselling book *A Brief History of Time*.

Chico Mendes

Jane Goodall

Stephen Hawking

1 Who tries/tried to save trees?
_____ and _____
2 Who was born in the 13ᵗʰ Century?

_____
3 Who tries to save animals?

_____
4 Who fights for democracy?

_____
5 Who is a famous scientist?

_____
6 Who won a prize?

_____

B Imagine you meet one of these people. Write two questions to ask him/her.

_____

_____

2 GRAMMAR: simple past with *when* clauses

A Put the words in the correct order to form sentences with *when*.

1 When / took / Sam / got home, / a shower / he / .

_____

2 Danuta / speak English / she / learned to / when / was / four / .

_____

3 the Opera House / they / saw / Mike and Patty / when / visited / Sydney / .

_____

4 she / Emi / was 16, / to the U.S.A. / When / went / .

_____

5 working / started / he / when / was 21 / Sonny / .

_____

6 were 18 / Alannah and Kacey / they / went / backpacking / when / .

_____

B Rewrite each pair of sentences to form one sentence, using a *when* clause. Use the correct punctuation.

1 I saw the crocodile. I screamed.

_____

2 Rosa got her first bicycle. She was 12 years old.

_____

3 We went to India. We visited the Taj Mahal.

_____

4 Gustav graduated from college. His parents gave him a graduation party.

_____

5 Sarah learned to speak Portuguese. She lived in Brazil.

_____

WATCH OUT!

✗ When he was 23 years old Pietro got married.

✓ _____

3 VOCABULARY: life events

A 🎧 36 Listen to a description of the life of the writer Isabel Allende. Number the events in the correct order.

☐ She had her daughter Paula.
☐ She had her son Nicolás.
☐ She became a U.S. citizen.
☐ She got married.
☐ She moved to Venezuela.
☐ She published her first novel.
☐ She left school.
☐ She was born in Lima, Peru.

B 🎧 **36** Complete the questions about Isabel Allende. Then listen again and match them to the answers.

1	_When did she leave school?_ ? (When / leave school)	a)	In 1962.
2	_____ ? (When / get married)	b)	In 2003.
3	_____ ? (When / become a U.S. citizen)	c)	In 1982.
4	_____ ? (When / have her second child)	d)	In 1963.
5	_____ ? (Where / grow up)	e)	In 1965.
6	_____ ? (When / born)	f)	In 1942.
7	_____ ? (Where / born)	g)	In 1958.
8	_____ ? (When / move to Venezuela)	h)	In 1975.
9	_____ ? (When / have her first child)	i)	In Chile.
10	_____ ? (When / publish her first novel)	j)	In Lima, Peru.

4 COMMUNICATION STRATEGY: taking time to think

A Complete the conversation with the phrases in the box.

I can't remember   I'm not sure, but   Just a second   Let me think   Oh, yeah   Well

Vicky: Mike, do you want to try this literary quiz?

Mike: (1) _____, I'm not good at literature, but why not … go ahead.

Vicky: OK, question one. Who wrote *The Merchant of Venice*?

Mike: (2) _____. That's easy—Shakespeare!

Vicky: Yes, that's right. And who wrote *The Old Man and the Sea*?

Mike: (3) _____. Was it Hemingway?

Vicky: Correct! And how many James Bond books did Ian Fleming write?

Mike: (4) _____ … I think there are ten.

Vicky: No, 14! And what's the name of the main character in *Twilight*?

Mike: (5) _____ … hmm, (6) _____.

Vicky: It's Bella.

B 🎧 **37** Listen and check your answers.

5 GRAMMAR: direct and indirect objects

A Complete the conversations with the correct object pronouns.

1 **A:** Did you invite Sally to your party?
   B: No, I don't know _____ very well.

2 **A:** Is that a new jacket?
   B: Yes, I bought _____ on sale last week.

3 **A:** When are Tony and Sue coming?
   B: I'm not sure. Let's call _____.

4 **A:** What are your plans for the weekend?
   B: We don't know yet. Ask _____ tomorrow!

5 **A:** Where did Bill and Angie go on vacation?
   B: I don't know. They didn't tell _____.

6 **A:** Is Pete back from his vacation?
   B: Yes, I saw _____ in class yesterday.

B Rewrite each sentence with direct and indirect object pronouns.

1 My mom bought the jacket for me for my birthday.
She _____ .

2 They gave my father the watch when he retired.
They _____ .

3 I sent an email to my sister this morning.
I _____ .

4 We showed our friends the new house last week.
We _____ .

5 My brother gave the book to me when I graduated.
He _____ .

6 My husband bought some flowers for me on our anniversary.
He _____ .

WATCH OUT!

✗ She gave to him a present.

✓ _____

6 VOCABULARY: historical events

A Write the simple past form of these verbs.

Base form	Simple past form	Base form	Simple past form
build		explore	
win		fight	
compose		invent	
discover		write	

B Complete the questions with one of the simple past verbs from Exercise A. Use each verb once only.

Test your
general knowledge

1 Who _____ the pyramids?

2 Who _____ the telephone in 1876?

3 Who _____ the song *Imagine*?

4 Who _____ gravity?

5 Who _____ the FIFA World Cup in 2012?

6 Who _____ *The Lord of the Rings*?

7 Who _____ the Trojans in the Trojan War?

8 Who _____ the Antarctic?

C Match the questions from Exercise B to the answers.

a) ☐ Spain

b) ☐ Ernest Shackleton

c) ☐ Isaac Newton

d) ☐ J.R.R. Tolkien

e) ☐ John Lennon

f) ☐ the ancient Egyptians

g) ☐ the Achaeans

h) ☐ Alexander Graham Bell

Listen and write

A 🎧 38 **Listen to a movie critic and answer the questions.**

1 Does the movie critic recommend the movie?
_____

2 What movie genre is it?
_____

3 What didn't women usually do at that time?
_____

B 🎧 38 **Listen again and complete the sentences.**

a) The movie is called *Becoming Jane,* and it's about the life of the _____ Jane Austen.

b) Jane Austen was born in _____.

c) The story in the movies starts when Jane began _____.

d) Her family wanted Jane _____.

e) But Jane _____ with a poor lawyer.

f) It's a romantic and _____ movie.

C **Match the sentences in Exercise B to these headings. Then put the headings in the correct order.**

1 ☐ Main character
2 ☐ Change in the storyline
3 ☐ Writer's opinion of movie
4 ☐ Development of storyline
5 ☐ Introduction to the story
6 ☐ Title and main idea of story

Over to You

D **Decide if the movie adjectives in the box are positive or negative, or both, and write them in the table.**

boring enjoyable exciting fascinating fast-moving funny happy imaginative predictable scary slow unpredictable

Positive	Negative	Both

E **Think of a movie or book you want to recommend to a friend. Using key words only, make some notes about it using the headings in Exercise C.**

F ✏ **In your notebook, write your recommendation. Use the headings in Exercise C and your notes in Exercise E to help you. Think about the structure and vocabulary.**

WRITING TUTOR

I read/saw … when …
It was …
The main characters were …
I liked/didn't like …
This was a time when …
The story begins when …
The movie is about …

DOWN TIME

A Look at the letters in the boxes, and spell out words from the unit.

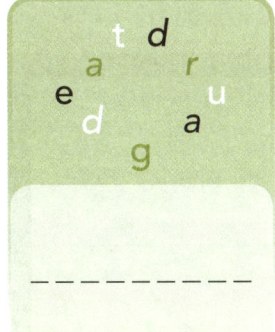

_ _ _ _ _ _ _ _ _

_ _ _ _ _ _ _

_ _ _ _ _ _ _ _

_ _ _ _ _ _ _ _

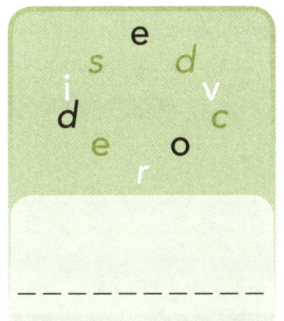

_ _ _ _ _ _ _ _ _ _

_ _ _ _ _

B Solve the brain teasers.

1. A family took a trip.
   – Mom sat behind her daughter.
   – Dad sat next to Mom.
   – the brother read a newspaper.
   Who drove the car?

2. There are 40 students in your class, but only a quarter of them came to class on time. Later on, 15 students came, but a third of those 15 left to go to lunch.
   How many students remained?

3. *Cruise Line* cruises has 3,500 places available. Different travel companies made 1,270 reservations in total on the first day. A group of graduates reserved 640 spaces on the second day, and two other agencies reserved 370 spaces each.
   How many spaces are left for the cruise?

UNIT 12　IN THE NEAR FUTURE

1 GRAMMAR: present progressive as future

A Look at Pete's plans for the week. Circle T (true) or F (false).

Sunday	Thursday
1 p.m. Lunch with my sister	1 p.m. Meet Liz for lunch at Brown's café
Monday	Friday
	9 p.m. Dancing with Daniela
Tuesday	Saturday
7 p.m. Go to the movies with Anna	10:30 a.m. Soccer with Andy and Jim
	7 p.m. Meet Jerry and Amy for dinner
Wednesday	NOTES

1 Pete and Liz are going dancing on Friday. *T / F*
2 Pete is having lunch with his sister on Sunday. *T / F*
3 Pete is going to the movies on Monday. *T / F*
4 Pete is playing soccer with Andy and Jim on Saturday morning. *T / F*

B Look at Pete's calendar again. Complete the sentences with the present progressive.

1 **A:** What _____ on Tuesday night?
   B: He's going to the movies.
2 **A:** Who _____ to the movies with?
   B: With Anna.
3 **A:** Where _____ Liz for lunch?
   B: At Brown's Café.
4 **A:** What time _____ Jerry and Amy on Saturday?
   B: At 7 p.m.
5 **A:** _____ soccer on Saturday morning?
   B: Yes, he is.
6 **A:** _____ anything on Monday night?
   B: No, he isn't.

WATCH OUT!

(X) Do you go to the movies tomorrow night?

(✓) _____

C There is one mistake in each sentence. Rewrite the sentences correctly.

1 What you are doing tomorrow night? _____
2 They watching a soccer game on Saturday. _____
3 Are your friend staying home this weekend? _____
4 They eat out in a Chinese restaurant tonight. _____
5 I am study for an exam tonight. _____
6 They not are working here next week. _____
7 We are visit my parents tonight. _____

2 LISTENING: understanding the main idea

A 🎧 39 Listen and decide which picture matches the main idea of the conversation. Circle the correct number.

1

2

B 🎧 39 Listen again and write down any key words about Jim's vacation.

_____

_____

C 🎧 39 Look at your key words and answer these questions. Then listen again and check your answers.

1 Where is Jim going for his vacation?

_____

2 What is Jim planning to do on his vacation?

_____

3 What is his ideal type of vacation?

_____

4 What does his friend think about his vacation?

_____

3 VOCABULARY: phrases with *go*

A Label the pictures using the phrases in the box.

go out   go out to eat   go out of town

1 _____

2 _____

3 _____

B 🎧 40 Listen to the conversations. What are the people doing? Use verbs with *go*.

1 *They are* _____

2 _____

3 _____

4 _____

4 GRAMMAR: *going to*

A Complete the sentences with *going to* and the verbs in parentheses.

1 I am planning to go to Italy. I _____ (*improve*) my Italian.
2 Tito wants to buy a car. But first he _____ (*learn*) how to drive.
3 Tomorrow is Uma's birthday. Her sister _____ (*bake*) a cake for her.
4 We don't have any money. We _____ (*not do*) anything this weekend.
5 Gino and Sam have an exam tomorrow. They _____ (*not go out*) tonight.

B Complete the questions with *going to* and the verbs in parentheses. Use the *you* form. Then complete the short answers.

1 A: Where _____ (*go*)?
  B: To Italy.
2 A: What _____ (*do*) there?
  B: Visit art galleries and learn about art.
3 A: Who _____ (*go*) with?
  B: With my girlfriend.
4 A: How long _____ (*stay*) there?
  B: For two months.
5 A: _____ (*study*) Italian?
  B: Yes, I _____.
6 A: _____ (*study*) Italian, too?
  B: No, she _____. She is going to study fashion design.

C Read the descriptions and write what these people are going to do with phrases in the box.

| be a lawyer get up earlier go running go to China |
| read magazines in English save money study harder |

1 Mary is in law school.
  She *is going to be a lawyer*.
2 Frank doesn't have enough money to buy a car.
  He _____.
3 I want to learn Chinese.
  I _____.
4 Elizabeth's grades are not good.
  She _____.
5 Frank and Julia are always late for work.
  They _____.
6 We want to exercise more.
  We _____.
7 They want to learn English.
  They _____.

WATCH OUT!

✗ They going to go out tonight.
✓ _____

5 VOCABULARY: intentions

A 🔊 **41** Listen to Toshi and Pete talking about what they are going to start and stop doing. Complete the table.

	Toshi	Pete
Start		
Stop		

B Complete the sentences about Toshi and Pete.

1 Toshi is going to start _____ and stop _____ .
2 Pete is going to stop _____ and start _____ .
3 Toshi and Pete are both going to start _____ .

6 WRITING: sequencing and connecting ideas

A Raul wants to be a movie director like the man in the picture. Number the steps in the best order.

- ☐ buy a video camera
- ☐ enter a movie competition
- ☐ take a course in movie directing
- ☐ make a short movie
- ☐ start saving money
- ☐ write a movie script
- ☐ stop spending money on clothes and CDs

B Write the steps using sequencing words like *first*, *then*, *next*, *after that*, and *finally* to connect your ideas.

Raul wants to be a movie director. This is his plan. First, he's going to …

_____
_____
_____
_____
_____
_____

C Read the text that you wrote in Exercise B. Check your spelling and punctuation carefully.

Read and write

A Read the website and check (✓) the activities you want to do in the future.

THINGS TO DO BEFORE I'M 50

A few years ago, I realized that there were many things that I didn't do in my 20s and 30s. I like to make plans, so I wrote a list of things I want to do before I'm 50. For example, I'm going to learn to scuba dive so I can see the coral reef in the Caribbean. I didn't learn a foreign language in college because I chose to study art. Now, I'm going to learn Spanish. I didn't travel much when I was young because my family preferred taking vacations in Florida. Next year, I want to go somewhere far away and very different, so maybe Japan.

You can start your own list, too. If you need some inspiration, here are some of my ideas.

- [ ] ride something bigger than a horse (an elephant? a camel?)
- [ ] visit all the continents
- [ ] cross a country on public transportation
- [ ] fly in a hot-air balloon
- [ ] learn another language
- [ ] do a bungee jump
- [ ] learn to ski
- [ ] learn to scuba dive
- [ ] learn to dance the tango
- [ ] do volunteer work
- [ ] climb a volcano
- [ ] learn how to make a national dish
- [ ] eat something exotic
- [ ] attend a music festival
- [ ] visit the birthplace of an important person

B Look at these example sentences from the text. Which word introduces a consequence? Which word introduces a reason? Find and <u>underline</u> other sentences in the text which explain a reason or a consequence.

I like to make plans, so I wrote a list …
I didn't learn a foreign language … because I chose to study art.

Over to You

C Make a list of things that you are going to do in the next ten years.

_____
_____
_____
_____
_____

WRITING TUTOR

I'm interested in … so …
I like … because / so …
I want to … so …
I'm going to … because …
Now, / Next year, / In two years, I'm going to …

D ✎ Choose five things from your list in Exercise C, and, in your notebook, write a short text about why you are going to do each thing.

DOWN TIME

A Take the trivia quiz. Circle the correct answer.

1 Who married Javier Bardem in 2010?
- a) Salma Hayek
- b) Penélope Cruz
- c) Scarlett Johansson

2 Which nationality was Mozart?
- a) Austrian
- b) German
- c) Russian

3 Where were the 2008 Olympic® Games?
- a) Great Britain
- b) South Africa
- c) China

4 Which famous singer worked at Dunkin' Donuts?
- a) Madonna
- b) Taylor Swift
- c) Pink

5 Who wrote the *Twilight* series?
- a) J.K. Rowling
- b) Robert Pattinson
- c) Stephenie Meyer

6 In which century did baseball start in the U.S.A.?
- a) 18th
- b) 20th
- c) 19th

7 Which movie didn't win an Academy Award® for best movie?
- a) *The Artist*
- b) *Midnight in Paris*
- c) *The King's Speech*

8 Which female artist had a hit with the song *Umbrella*?
- a) Beyoncé
- b) Rihanna
- c) Katy Perry

9 Which is the most successful album of all time?
- a) Pink Floyd: *The Wall*
- b) Michael Jackson: *Thriller*
- c) The Beatles: *The White Album*

10 Where did Usain Bolt win three gold medals?
- a) Beijing
- b) London
- c) Paris

11 Where was Ricky Martin born?
- a) Mexico
- b) Cuba
- c) Puerto Rico

12 Which country founded New Orleans?
- a) Spain
- b) France
- c) Belgium

Audio script

UNIT 1

Track 01

1. Can you spell that?
2. Can you speak more slowly?
3. How do you say that in English?
4. Can you repeat that, please?
5. What does that mean?
6. Can you help me?

Track 02

HC = Hotel clerk; MC = Ms Cardoza

HC: Excuse me. Can you spell your last name, please?
MC: Yes, it's C-A-R-D-O-Z-A.
HC: Thank you. And what's your phone number?
MC: It's (555) 214-0091.
HC: OK. You're in room 235. Here's your room key.
MC: Thanks.
HC: You're welcome. Enjoy your stay.

Track 03

1. My birthday is on October ninth.
2. This is my first day in this class.
3. Next Wednesday is November the twenty-fifth.
4. The last day of August is the thirty-first.
5. My birthday is April seventeenth.
6. Today is the twelfth.

Track 04

Hi, my name is Lucy. My last name is Cheng. That's C-H-E-N-G. I'm from Shanghai in China. I'm 20 years old. I would like to know some information about your English course. Can you please call me back? My number is (555) 841-0789. That's (555) 841-0789. Thank you.

Track 05

J = John; K = Kate

J: Barton College. Can I help you?
K: Hello. I want to take an evening class please.
J: OK. First I need to take some information. What is your first name, please?
K: Kate. My name is Kate.
J: And what is your last name?
K: It's Robinson.
J: Can you spell that?
K: R-O-B-I-N-S-O-N.
J: And how old are you, Kate?
K: I'm 19.
J: When is your birthday?
K: In December, December the seventh.
J: Can you repeat that?
K: Of course, it's December the seventh.
J: And finally, what's your email address?
K: It's kate192@mail.com.
J: Great. So what class do you want to take?
K: Well, I'm interested in …

UNIT 2

Track 06

Which occupations are interesting? Hmm … I think being a doctor is very interesting. You can help people. You can discover new medicines. That's my number one. And number two is engineer. Being an engineer is interesting because you can build new things like bridges and tunnels. I think firefighter is my number three. It's exciting, but very dangerous. I don't like this job. I think police officer is number four because it's hard work and dangerous. It's not a lot of fun. And my number five is taxi driver because driving a taxi is not interesting. But my number six is writer. You don't talk to anyone. You just stay on the computer all day. So, yes, 1 doctor, 2 engineer, 3 firefighter, 4 police officer, 5 taxi driver, and 6 writer.

Track 07

This is my family tree. That's me on the end. My name's Marta. And there's my mom and my dad. My mom is Bianca, and my dad is Hector. That's my sister. Her name is Rita. She's married. That's her husband, Martin, and their two children, Lisa and Sasha – that's Sasha on the right. Juan is my brother. He isn't married. Oh, yes, and the most important person – that's my grandma, Clara.

Track 08

Brenda Jones is a lawyer. She lives in Seattle. Brenda starts work at 8:30 a.m. She says her job is very exciting. Her husband isn't a lawyer. He's an engineer. Their daughter is a student.

UNIT 3

Track 09

A = Andrew; B = Bettina

A: Hi, Bettina. Can I ask you some questions for a survey?
B: Sure! Go ahead.
A: Do you listen to music?
B: Yes, I do. I listen to country music. I really like country music.
A: And do you play the guitar?
B: No, I don't.
A: Do your parents listen to music a lot?
B: No, they don't.
A: Do you buy a lot of CDs?
B: No, I don't. I buy MP3s online.
A: Great! That's all. Thanks a lot!
B: Sure, no problem.

Track 10

1. Everyone likes Marisa because she tells a lot of good jokes and makes people laugh.
2. Lucia doesn't like big parties with a lot of people. She's nervous about meeting new people. She prefers to go out with just one or two friends.
3. Eddie likes to meet new people. He likes to talk with people and he isn't shy.
4. Patrick is a kind person. He helps people. He opens the door, or carries heavy things for them.
5. Andrea is a good friend. When life is difficult, she's always there to help you.
6. Kyle likes to have a good time and has a lot of friends – everyone likes him.

Track 11

I = Interviewer; A = Alex; J = Jenny

I: Today, I have Alex Hartford and his sister Jenny in the studio. You know them as brother and sister pop group *Generation Y*. Alex and Jenny, welcome.
A/J: Thanks.
I: So, we know about your music, but tell us a little about you. Are you similar?
A: No way! We're very different. I'm a pretty shy guy. I don't really have a lot of friends – well, I have a few good friends, but that's it.
I: And what about you, Jenny?
J: I'm the party animal in our family!
A: Yeah, she's very sociable and popular. Probably because she's really funny.

J: Aw, that's so loyal of you, Alex!

I: OK! And tell us a little about your daily life.

A: Well, we're musicians, so every morning we go to our studio to write new songs. After we finish, I usually practice my guitar.

J: And I usually go to the gym to work out in the afternoon.

I: And what do you do in your free time? Do you do the same things?

J: Not at all. On weekends, I like to see friends and go to parties.

A: I like to see my friends, but we don't go to parties. We usually do something quiet like go bowling or watch a movie.

I: Sounds like a great life! Well thanks, Alex and Jenny …

UNIT 4

Track 12

1 Hurry up, it's twenty after eight.
2 It's nine o'clock on Tuesday, August twenty-second.
3 **A:** Excuse me, what time is it?
   B: It's a quarter after six.
4 The time is eleven forty-five p.m.
5 Come on, it's five-thirty. Time to go home!
6 It's seven-fifteen, wake up!

Track 13

My name is Amanda. I'm an architect. On Mondays, I go to the office to talk with clients about new designs. Then I talk about the designs with my team. On Tuesdays, I visit one of our new building projects to help with any problems. The rest of the week I work from home. On Tuesday afternoons, I work out in the gym. On Wednesday nights, I watch my brother's children because he goes to night school. On Thursday nights, I usually go bowling with my friends. I always go dancing on Friday nights. On Saturdays, I go shopping, and on Sundays, I go for a walk or ride my bike.

Track 14

Hi. My name is Greg. I'm a businessman. On Mondays, I usually stay home and work on the computer. The rest of the week I work in the office. I finish work at about three o'clock. On Tuesday nights, I work out in the gym. On Wednesday nights, I have dinner with a friend. On Thursday nights, I usually stay home. On Friday nights, I go shopping. On Saturdays, I go to the movies and see friends, and on Sundays, I stay home and I practice the guitar.

UNIT 5

Track 15

A: So, what places can we visit when I come to see you tomorrow?

B: We can go to the art gallery and the museum, that's for sure. They're both really interesting. How about shopping? Do you want to go to the mall?

A: No! I hate shopping malls. I want to go for a walk in the park, and then maybe go to a café for lunch?

B: OK. That sounds great. We can have lunch in the museum—the café there is really good—and then go for a walk in the park.

A: Great!

Track 16

1 **A:** Excuse me, where's the museum?
   B: You go straight ahead and take the second left.
   A: I see. Straight ahead and take the third left?
   B: No, not the third left, the second left.
   A: Thanks.
   B: No problem.

2 **A:** Excuse me, how do I get to the shopping mall?
   B: You take the first right. Then go straight ahead.
   A: First left. Then go straight ahead?
   B: No, first right, then go straight ahead.
   A: Thank you.
   B: You're welcome.

3 **A:** Excuse me, how do I get to the train station?
   B: Turn left here, and then take the third right.
   A: Go straight here, and then take the third right?
   B: No, turn left here and then take the third right.
   A: OK. Thanks.

Track 17

Edinburgh, the capital of Scotland, is an interesting city. Stay in the old part of town and visit its beautiful buildings and historical monuments. There are many castles in Scotland, but don't miss Edinburgh Castle because there you can learn about Scottish kings and queens, and see the crown jewels. At night, try the walking tour. This way you can visit famous places from the *Harry Potter* movies. It starts at 10 p.m. in the cemetery. Don't forget your camera, and bring warm clothes. In August, there is a famous international arts event. It's called the Edinburgh Festival. There are comedy, dance, music, and theater shows all day and night. Remember to book a hotel early because there are over one million visitors during that month.

UNIT 6

Track 18

1 exciting
2 stressful
3 relaxing
4 unhealthy
5 boring
6 green

Track 19

My younger sister Donna eats a lot of fast food. She watches TV all day and doesn't do any exercise.
My brother Mark travels all over the world for his job. And he meets lots of famous people.
My brother's wife Karen eats only organic fruit and vegetables. She rides a bike to work every day.
My dad never worries about anything. He likes to read and listen to music, and he always has time to talk with his children.
My mom works in a bank. She works late every night and is always worried about her work.
And me … well, I go to school, I come home, I do my homework, I watch TV. Every day is the same old routine really. My lifestyle isn't very exciting!

Track 20

1 I'm twenty-nine years old.
2 The time is five after four.
3 My phone number is five five five—three one five—seven zero eight two.
4 This building dates from nineteen forty-nine.
5 My birth date is April seventeenth, nineteen ninety-three.

Track 21

Hi. My name is Leonardo Oliveira. My account number is 5421390426. My ID number is 11488566. I'm calling about this month's statement, which is $526. There's a $59 charge, but I don't know what it's about. Please call me back. My number is (555) 431-3237.

UNIT 7

Track 22

1 Elena can play the piano.
2 Peter can dance.
3 I can't sing.
4 We can't drive.

Track 23

B = Bella; R = Ricky

B: Ricky, can you help me with this questionnaire?
R: Sure.
B: Can you play a sport?
R: Yes, I can play tennis. Can you?
B: No, I'm not good at sports. Can you speak another language?
R: Yes, I can. I can speak German.
B: Oh! I can speak German, too. Can you cook?
R: Yes, I can. I can cook spaghetti. Very delicious.
B: Mmm, yum. That sounds great because I can't cook anything. How about some spaghetti for dinner tonight?

Track 24

Chloe is very talented. She can play all kinds of musical instruments, including the piano. She's also good at singing and can sing opera as well as traditional songs.
Alicia is good at all kinds of sports. Her favorite sports are karate and soccer. She's also good at dancing, especially salsa and merengue.
Tony is good at languages. He can speak Russian and German. And he can also cook Russian food.

Track 25

1 A: Can you play any musical instruments?
  B: Yes, I can play the guitar and the piano.
  A: Wow. That's amazing!
2 A: Can you speak any foreign languages?
  B: Yes, I can speak Esperanto.
  A: Oh, really?
3 A: Can you dance?
  B: No, but I can sing.
  A: Oh, that's great!

Track 26

1 Hi, I'm Sara. I love music. I'm friendly and generous. I can play the guitar, and I can sing. I'm good at making friends.
2 Um, hi, I'm Dominic. Um, I'm smart and honest. I can speak English and Spanish. I can play chess. I like reading and doing quiet activities.
3 My name's Brianna. I'm very patient and reliable. I can cook very well and can make delicious sushi. I like doing new things.
4 Hi. I'm Dean. I'm very athletic, and I like sports. I can play basketball very well. I like doing exciting things.

UNIT 8

Track 27

1 A: Can I help you?
  B: Yes. How much is that sweatshirt?
  A: It's $49.95.
2 A: Excuse me. How much are those shoes?
  B: They're $112.
3 A: Are these T-shirts $6?
  B: Yes, usually they are, but today they're on sale for only $3.50 each.
4 A: Excuse me. How much is this shirt?
  B: It's $29.50.
  A: Thank you.

Track 28

A: Hello and welcome to *Guess the Price!* We show you things, and you have to guess the price. The contestant with the closest guess wins the item! First, we have this great compact refrigerator.
B: Hmm, I think it's $299.
C: I think it's more. I say $350.
D: I don't think it's very expensive. How about $230?
A: OK, well, the real price is … $250! So you win, number three. Congratulations! Our next item is this amazing flat screen TV. How much is it?
B: I say $599.
C: Oh, no, I think it's $550.
D: I think it's more expensive. $700?
A: And the real price is … $550! So you win, number two. Congratulations! Our next item is this beautiful necklace. How much is it?
B: My guess is $1,000.
C: I say, hmm, $1,500.
D: I think it's $2,000.
A: And the real price is … $1,000! So you win, number one. Congratulations! See you again next week on *Guess the Price!*

Track 29

1 expensive
2 compact
3 versatile
4 powerful
5 user-friendly

Track 30

1 You can use this to send emails and messages, listen to music, surf the internet – and a lot of other things.
2 This is a luxury product. It isn't cheap, but the sound quality is excellent.
3 This player is so easy to use! You won't believe how great it is.
4 You can put this in your shirt pocket. It's less than two inches wide and weighs just a few ounces.
5 This version has a higher-speed connection than our previous model.

UNIT 9

Track 31

A: Good afternoon. Could I speak to Mr. Brown, please?
B: I'm sorry. He isn't here right now. Would you like to leave a message?
A: Yes, please. Could you ask him to call me back? My name's Mike Vodel, and my number is 460-0131.
B: Yes, of course.
A: Thank you.
B: You're welcome.

Track 32

W = Waiter; B = Brian; J = Jessica

W: Hi. Are you ready to order?
B: Yes, I'm ready. How about you, Jessica?
J: Yes, I think so. I'd like mushroom soup first, please. And then I'd like the chicken salad.
W: Mushroom soup … and chicken salad. OK. And would you like anything to drink with that?
J: Just a glass of water, please.
B: And I'd like the spinach and cheese pie to start with … and spaghetti with meatballs.
W: OK … spinach and cheese pie … and … spaghetti with meatballs. Anything to drink?
B: No, I'll have coffee later, with my dessert.
W: Would you like to order your desserts now?
J: Yes, I'd like apple pie with ice cream, please.

B: And I'd like cheesecake and a black coffee.

W: Right. One apple pie with ice cream and one cheesecake and a black coffee. I'll be right back with your appetizers.

Track 33

P = Presenter; A = Antonio Mereda

P: Good morning and welcome to *Healthy Eating*. Today we have Chef Antonio Mereda with us. Welcome to the show.

A: Thank you. It's a pleasure to be here.

P: So, what do you want to make today?

A: Well, today, Mike, I'd like to make my favorite salad: spinach and strawberry.

P: Wow, that sounds good. What do you need for it?

A: Well, you need some spinach, and a few strawberries of course. You also need some nuts and some butter. And for the dressing you need oil, vinegar, paprika, and onion.

P: OK. And how do you make it?

A: First, you melt the butter over medium heat, then add the nuts. You need to cook these for about one minute. Put the spinach, strawberries, and nuts in a bowl. Combine the oil, vinegar, paprika, and onion, and pour this over the salad.

P: Sounds fantastic! Well, thank you, Antonio.

UNIT 10

Track 34

A: What did you do on Friday night?

B: I went out for dinner.

A: Where did you go?

B: To the new Thai restaurant. It's fantastic.

A: Oh, wow! Did you have a good time?

B: Yes, it was great.

A: Who did you go with?

B: With my girlfriend.

A: And how was the food?

B: Oh, fantastic. I love Thai food.

A: And was it very expensive?

B: Mmm, not too bad actually …

Track 35

1   **A:** So, how was your exam, Sarah?

     B: Oh, it was OK, you know …

     A: Not too good, huh?

     B: Well, the first few questions were OK, but then I got confused.

     A: Was it more difficult than you thought?

     B: Everyone said the exam was very hard. I'm sure I failed.

     A: Well, better luck next time.

     B: Thanks!

2   **A:** Hey, Andy, how was your trip?

     B: Amazing! We had a really good time.

     A: Were you in the mountains?

     B: Yes, there was a lot of snow. It was great!

     A: Did you go out on the slopes every day?

     B: Yes, we did. I only fell over twice!

     A: Sounds like a good trip!

3   **A:** Simon, how's it going?

     B: Not bad, how about you?

     A: Great! How was the game?

     B: Oh, I'm exhausted. I stayed up all night. We were celebrating.

     A: Oh, so you won?

     B: You bet! Two-nothing!

     A: Sounds like it was a good game.

B: Yes, you should come and watch next time. I can get some tickets for you.

A: Cool! I'd like that!

UNIT 11

Track 36

Isabel Allende was born in Lima, Peru in 1942, but she grew up in Chile. After she left school in 1958, she worked as a translator and journalist. She got married in 1962, and she had her first child, Paula, in 1963. The family moved to Europe and in 1965, they returned to Chile, and Allende had her second child, Nicolás, there that year. In 1975, she moved to Venezuela where she got a job as a TV host. In 1982, she published her first novel *The House of the Spirits*. Now her novels are famous all over the world, and she is head of a foundation to help protect the rights of women and children. In 2003, she became a U.S. citizen, and she now lives in California.

Track 37

A: Mike, do you want to try this literary quiz?

B: Well, I'm not good at literature, but why not … go ahead.

A: OK, question one. Who wrote *The Merchant of Venice*?

B: Oh, yeah. That's easy — Shakespeare!

A: Yes, that's right. And who wrote *The Old Man and the Sea*?

B: Just a second. Was it Hemingway?

A: Correct! And how many James Bond books did Ian Fleming write?

B: I'm not sure, but I think there are ten.

A: No, 14! And what's the name of the main character in *Twilight*?

B: Let me think … hmm … I can't remember.

A: It's Bella.

Track 38

Hello, everyone! Today we have a great movie to recommend, called *Becoming Jane* … It's a movie about the life of the English author, Jane Austen.

Jane Austen was born in 1775, at a time when women got married to help their family and didn't usually get jobs or earn money. The story in the movie starts when Jane was a young woman and started writing, but also at a time when her family wanted her to get married. Her mother wanted her to marry a rich man. But Jane fell in love with a poor lawyer. The story is about their romance and the dilemma they faced. I loved this movie as it was both romantic and sad. I say go out and rent it today!

UNIT 12

Track 39

A: Hi, Jim. You look busy!

B: Yes, I'm going on vacation tomorrow. I need clothes for walking in the jungle!

A: Wow! Where are you going?

B: I'm going to Borneo with a group of friends. First, we're doing a trek through the jungle, and then we're going on a river trip to take pictures of wild animals – crocodiles and iguanas and that kind of thing.

A: That sounds amazing! But, isn't it dangerous?

B: Yes … But, that's my ideal vacation – exploring unusual and exciting places far away from civilization.

A: I think that's great, but … I prefer to stay in a hotel near the beach! Adventure trips aren't really my kind of thing.

Track 40

1 **A:** Is that your new bike? It looks great!
   B: Yes, I can't wait to try it out.
   A: OK. Let's go this weekend.
2 **A:** I really need some new shoes.
   B: I think there's a sale on this Saturday.
   A: Great! Do you want to come with me?
3 **A:** Aren't you going in? The water's really warm!
   B: No, you go in. I'll lie here on the beach for a while.
   A: Go on! Come in with me!
   B: Oh, OK then.
4 **A:** I'd like to go with you, but my leg hurts.
   B: We're only going around the park for about half an hour, and we can go slowly if you want.
   A: OK. Hang on. I'll get my sneakers.

Track 41

P = Pete; T = Toshi

P: What resolutions are you going to make for next year, Toshi?

T: Um … well … I'm not very good at making resolutions, Pete, but … I'm definitely going to start bringing a packed lunch to work. I'm going to stop eating junk food like burgers and fries.

P: Good idea! I know what mine's going to be: I'm going to start riding my bike to work every day. It's healthy, and I could lose some weight, too. And I'm going to stop eating chocolate.

T: Now that's a resolution I couldn't keep. I love chocolate. But I'm going to stop drinking coffee. I'm going to start drinking green tea instead. It's healthier.

P: Green tea! Good idea. I'm going to do that, too.